Grammar Sense 3A

SECOND EDITION

SERIES DIRECTOR
and AUTHOR
Susan Kesner Bland

OXFORD
UNIVERSITY PRESS

OXFORD
UNIVERSITY PRESS

198 Madison Avenue
New York, NY 10016 USA

Great Clarendon Street, Oxford, OX2 6DP, United Kingdom

Oxford University Press is a department of the University of Oxford.
It furthers the University's objective of excellence in research, scholarship,
and education by publishing worldwide. Oxford is a registered trade
mark of Oxford University Press in the UK and in certain other countries

General Manager, American ELT: Laura Pearson
Publisher: Stephanie Karras
Associate Publishing Manager: Sharon Sargent
Managing Editor: Alex Ragan
Director, ADP: Susan Sanguily
Executive Design Manager: Maj-Britt Hagsted
Electronic Production Manager: Julie Armstrong
Senior Designer: Yin Ling Wong
Image Manager: Trisha Masterson

Publishing and Editorial Management: hyphen S.A.

ISBN: 978 0 19 448917 1 Student Book 3A with Online Practice pack
ISBN: 978 0 19 448907 2 Student Book 3A as pack component
ISBN: 978 0 19 448928 7 Online Practice as pack component

Printed in China

This book is printed on paper from certified and well-managed sources

ACKNOWLEDGEMENTS

*Although every effort has been made to trace and contact copyright holders before
publication, this has not been possible in some cases. We apologize for any apparent
infringement of copyright and if notified, the publisher will be pleased to rectify any
errors or omissions at the earliest opportunity.*

*The authors and publisher are grateful to those who have given permission to
reproduce the following extracts and adaptations of copyright material:* pp. 4–5.
"You Snooze, You Win at Today's Workplace." This article first appeared
in *The Christian Science Monitor* on June 17, 1999, and is reproduced and
adapted with permission. © 1999 The Christian Science Publishing
Society. All rights reserved; pp. 28–29. Adapted from: *A Night To Remember*
by Walter Lord, © 1955, 1976 by Walter Lord. Reprinted by permission of
Henry Holt and Company, LLC.; pp. 78–79. "The Questions That Stump The
Scientists." Adapted from *Newsweek*, January 19, 1998 © 1998 Newsweek,
Inc. All rights reserved. Reprinted by permission; pp. 168–169. "The Really
Early Birds: A new theory explains how the first feathered creatures to fly
may have gotten off the ground," by Thomas Hayden. From Newsweek,
May 17, 1999 © 1999 Newsweek, Inc. All rights reserved. Reprinted by
permission.

Illustrations by: Thanos Tsilis (hyphen): 14, 37, 55, 73, 111, 133, 179, 290,
292; Alexandros Tzimeros / SmartMagna (hyphen): 11, 12, 22, 42, 44, 57,
84, 91, 108, 129, 135, 175, 224, 231, 256, 285, 334, 337, 349, 357.

*We would also like to thank the following for permission to reproduce the following
photographs*: Devation - Edwin Verbruggen / www.shutterstock.com,
Andreas Gradin / shutterstock.com, homydesign / www.shutterstock.com,
marekuliasz / www.shutterstock.com, Travel Ink / Getty Images, Cover l to
r and interior; Marcin Krygier / iStockphoto, Front matter and back cover
(laptop); Freitag / Corbis, pg. 4; GoGo Images Corporation / Alamy, pg. 8;
Rune Hellestad / Corbis, pg. 23; Tanya Constantine / Blend Images / Corbis,
pg. 25; Ralph White / Corbis, pg. 28; Deborah Feingold / Corbis, pg. 50;
David Matthew Walters / Gerald Celente, pg. 51; Corel / OUPpicturebank,
pg. 78; Paul Fleet / OUPpicturebank, pg. 99; Geray Sweeney / Corbis,
pg. 102; Photodisc / OUPpicturebank, pg. 119; Anthony West / Corbis,
pg. 122; New York Times Co. / Contributor / Getty, pg. 126;
Phase4Photography / Shutterstock, pg. 146; AF Archive / Alamy, pg. 150;
Tom & Dee Ann McCarthy / Corbis, pg. 157 (outdoor event); Serge Kozak
/ Corbis, pg. 157 (people throwing papers); Sally A. Morgan / Ecoscene
/ Corbis, pg. 168; Jonathan Blair / Corbis, pg. 172; Chris Howes / Wild
Places Photography / Alamy, pg. 177; Corbis / OUPpicturebank, pg. 192
(happiness); UpperCut / OUPpicturebank, pg. 192 (anger); Chris Carroll /
Corbis, pg. 192 (surprise); Eugene Duran / Corbis, pg. 192 (fear); Charles
O'Rear / Corbis, pg. 196; galvezrc / Demotix / Corbis, pg. 204; Anna Clopet
/ Corbis, pg. 209; Comstock / OUPpicturebank, pg. 212; JGI / Tom Grill
/ Blend Images / Corbis, pg. 220; Photodisc / OUPpicturebank, pg. 241;
Corbis/OUPpicturebank, pg. 251; Blaine Harrington III / Corbis, pg. 260;
Glowimages / Corbis, pg. 273 (spatula); StudioSource / Alamy, pg. 273
(crib); Bill Ross / Corbis, pg. 273 (iris); Bialy / Dorota i Bogdan / the food
passionate / Corbis, pg. 273 (octopus); Ned Therrien / Visuals Unlimited
/ Corbis, pg. 273 (elm); Ingram / OUPpicturebank, pg. 273 (calculator);
Photodisc / OUPpicturebank, pg. 273 (pineapple); OUP / OUPpicturebank,
pg. 273 (screwdriver); Ambrophoto / Shutterstock, pg. 280; Jonathan
Larsen / Diadem Images / Alamy, pg. 302; Anthony J. Causi / Icon SMI
/ Corbis, pg. 321; Bettmann / Corbis, pg. 352; Corbis / Corbis, pg. 353
(van Gogh); Sandro Vannini / Corbis, pg. 353 (Cleopatra); Renphoto /
iStockphoto, pg. 372; Photodisc / OUPpicturebank, pg. 389; Steve Prezant /
Corbis, pg. 392; Asia Images RF / OUPpicturebank, pg. 398; Kevin Peterson /
OUPpicturebank, pg. 405 (woman); Kevin Peterson / OUPpicturebank,
pg. 405 (man); Kevin Peterson / OUPpicturebank, pg. 406 (older
woman); Naho Yoshizawa / Aflo / Corbis, pg. 406 (man); Kevin Peterson /
OUPpicturebank, pg. 406 (woman).

Reviewers

*We would like to acknowledge the following
individuals for their input during the development
of the series:*

Marcia Adato, Delaware Technical and Community
College, DE
Donette Artenie, Georgetown University, DC
Alexander Astor, Hostos Community College/CUNY,
Bronx, NY
Nathalie Bailey, Lehman College, CUNY, NY
Jamie Beaton, Boston University, MA
Michael Berman, Montgomery College, MD
Linda Best, Kean University, NJ
Marcel Bolintiam, Kings Colleges, Los Angeles, CA
Houda Bouslama, Virtual University Tunis, Tunis, Tunisia
Nancy Boyer, Golden West College, Huntington Beach, CA
Glenda Bro, Mount San Antonio Community College, CA
Shannonine Caruana, Kean University, NJ
Sharon Cavusgil, Georgia State University, GA
Robin Rosen Chang, Kean University, NJ
Jorge Cordon, Colegio Internacional Montessori,
Guatemala
Magali Duignan, Augusta State University, GA
Anne Ediger, Hunter College, CUNY, NY
Begoña Escourdio, Colegio Miraflores, Naucalpan, Mexico
Marcella Farina, University of Central Florida, FL
Carol Fox, Oakton Community College, Niles, IL
Glenn S. Gardner, Glendale Community College,
Glendale, CA
Ruth Griffith, Kean University, NJ
Evalyn Hansen, Rogue Community College, Medford, OR
Liz Hardy, Rogue Community College, Medford, OR
Habiba Hassina, Virtual University Tunis, Tunis, Tunisia
Virginia Heringer, Pasadena City College, CA
Rocia Hernandez, Mexico City, Mexico
Kieran Hilu, Virginia Tech, VA
Rosemary Hiruma, California State University,
Long Beach, CA
Linda Holden, College of Lake County, Grayslake, IL
Elke Holtz, Escuela Sierra Nevada Interlomas,
Mexico City, Mexico
Kate de Jong, University of California, San Diego, CA
Gail Kellersberger, University of Houston-Downtown, ELI,
Houston, TX

Pamela Kennedy, Holyoke Community College, MA
Elis Lee, Glendale Community College, Glendale, CA
Patricia Lowy, State University of New York-New Paltz, NY
Jean McConochie, Pace University, NY
Karen McRobie, Golden Gate University, CA
Hafid Mekaoui, Al Akhawayn University, Ifrane, Morocco
Elizabeth Neblett, Union County College, NJ
Patricia Palermo, Kean University, NJ
Maria E. Palma, Colegio Lationamericano Bilingue,
Chihuahua, Mexico
Mary Peacock, Richland College, Dallas, TX
Dian Perkins, Wheeling High School, IL
Nancy Herzfeld-Pipkin, Grossmont College, El Cajon, CA
Kent Richmond, California State University,
Long Beach, CA
Ellen Rosen, Fullerton College, CA
Jessica Saigh, University of Missouri-St. Louis,
St. Louis, MO
Boutheina Lassadi-Sayadi, The Faculty of Humanities and
Social Sciences of Tunis, Tunis, Tunisia
Anne-Marie Schlender, Austin Community College-Rio
Grande, Austin, TX
Shira Seaman, Global English Academy, NY
Katharine Sherak, San Francisco State University, CA
Maxine Steinhaus, New York University, NY
Andrea Stewart, Houston Community College-Gulfton,
Houston, TX
Nancy Storer, University of Denver, CO
Veronica Struck, Sussex Community College, Newton, NJ
Frank Tang, New York University, NY
Claude Taylor, Baruch College, NY
Marshall Thomas, California State University,
Long Beach, CA
Christine Tierney, Houston Community College,
Houston, TX
Anthea Tillyer, Hunter College, CUNY, NY
Julie Un, Massasoit Community College, MA
Marvaette Washington, Houston Community College,
Houston, TX
Cheryl Wecksler, California State University,
San Marcos, CA
Teresa Wise, Associated Colleges of the South, GA

Contents

Welcome to Grammar Sense

A Sensible Solution to Learning Grammar

Grammar Sense Second Edition gives learners a true understanding of how grammar is used in authentic contexts.

  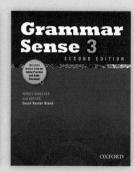 

With Grammar Sense Online Practice

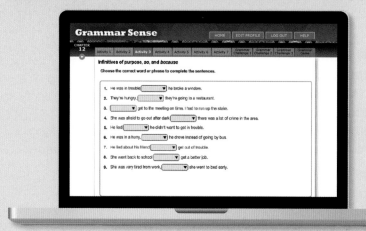

- **Student Solutions:** a **focus on Critical Thinking** for improved application of grammatical knowledge.

- **Writing Solutions:** a **Writing section in every chapter** encourages students to see the relevance of grammar in their writing.

- **Technology Solutions:** *Grammar Sense Online Practice* provides additional practice in an easy-to-use **online workbook**.

- **Assessment Solutions:** the Part Tests at the end of every section and the Grammar Sense Test Generators allow **ongoing assessment**.

Each chapter in *Grammar Sense Second Edition* **follows** this format.

The Grammar in Discourse section introduces the target grammar in its natural context via high-interest readings.

A GRAMMAR IN DISCOURSE

You Snooze, You Win at Today's Workplace

A1 Before You Read

 Discuss these questions.

How much sleep do you get each night? Do you usually get enough sleep? Why or why not? Do you ever take naps?

A2 Read

CD1 T2 Read this magazine article to find out how some businesses are helping their tired employees.

You Snooze, You Win at Today's Workplace

It's early afternoon and lunch is over. You're sitting at your desk and plowing through paperwork. Suddenly you're fighting to keep your eyes open. The
5 words on your computer are zooming in and out of focus, and your head is beginning to bob in all directions. A nap sounds good right about now—so does a couch or reclining armchair.

10 Well, a growing number of companies are beginning to accept the idea of sleeping on the job. No, it's not a dream. Employees are increasingly sleeping less and working longer
15 hours at the office. Some employers, therefore, are warming up to the idea that a midday nap helps increase productivity, creativity, and safety.

Some companies are now providing
20 tents in quiet areas of their offices. Each one contains a sleeping bag, a foam pad, an MP3 player, eye shades, and yes, an alarm clock. In Japan, some firms have "nightingale rooms"
25 where employees are encouraged to take "power naps," and nap salons are springing up around the globe in cities like London, Amsterdam, Tokyo, and New York.

fact, it sometimes leads
till, that doesn't stop
. according to Professor
und that "they're
r cars, in the bathroom,
oms. Others are trying to
in their cubicles.
the phone to their ear,
o write or read

Adapted from *The Christian Science Monitor*

bob: to move repeatedly up and down
cubicle: a small enclosed area
dismissal: telling an employee that he or she is fired
plow through: to force one's way through

productivity: the amount of work you can do in a certain time
snooze: to nap
warm up to: to begin to like

A3 After You Read

Write *T* for true or *F* for false for each statement.

___T__ 1. Tired workers produce fewer products.

_____ 2. Some employers provide special napping areas.

_____ 3. People need to sleep a total of five hundred hours a year.

_____ 4. One study shows that most adults get eight hours of sleep per night.

_____ 5. Most companies do not encourage napping.

_____ 6. Employees only nap at the office.

Exposure to **authentic readings** encourages awareness of the grammar in daily life: in textbooks, magazines, newspapers, websites, and so on.

Pre- and post-reading tasks help students understand the text.

The Form section(s) provides clear presentation of the target grammar, detailed notes, and thorough practice exercises.

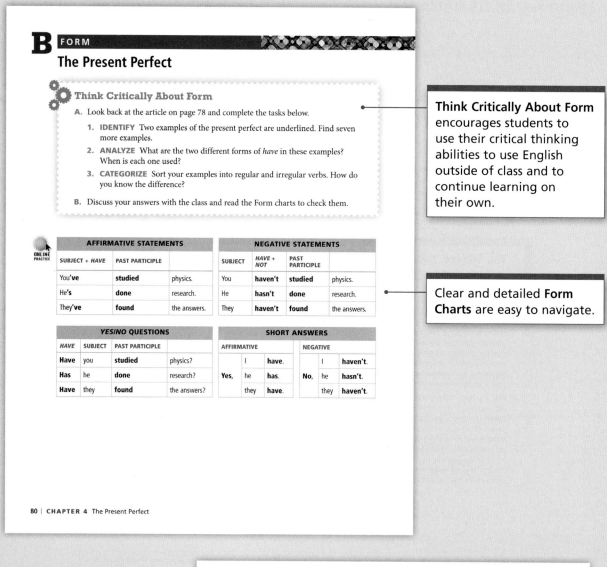

B FORM

The Present Perfect

Think Critically About Form

A. Look back at the article on page 78 and complete the tasks below.

1. **IDENTIFY** Two examples of the present perfect are underlined. Find seven more examples.

2. **ANALYZE** What are the two different forms of *have* in these examples? When is each one used?

3. **CATEGORIZE** Sort your examples into regular and irregular verbs. How do you know the difference?

B. Discuss your answers with the class and read the Form charts to check them.

Think Critically About Form encourages students to use their critical thinking abilities to use English outside of class and to continue learning on their own.

ONLINE PRACTICE

AFFIRMATIVE STATEMENTS		
SUBJECT + *HAVE*	PAST PARTICIPLE	
You**'ve**	**studied**	physics.
He**'s**	**done**	research.
They**'ve**	**found**	the answers.

NEGATIVE STATEMENTS			
SUBJECT	*HAVE* + NOT	PAST PARTICIPLE	
You	**haven't**	**studied**	physics.
He	**hasn't**	**done**	research.
They	**haven't**	**found**	the answers.

YES/NO QUESTIONS			
HAVE	SUBJECT	PAST PARTICIPLE	
Have	you	**studied**	physics?
Has	he	**done**	research?
Have	they	**found**	the answers?

SHORT ANSWERS					
AFFIRMATIVE			NEGATIVE		
	I	**have.**		I	**haven't.**
Yes,	he	**has.**	No,	he	**hasn't.**
	they	**have.**		they	**haven't.**

Clear and detailed **Form Charts** are easy to navigate.

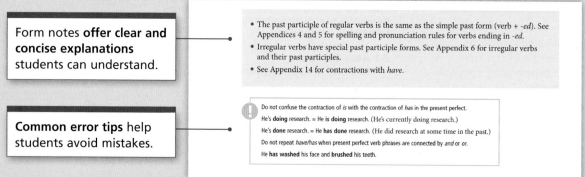

Form notes **offer clear and concise explanations** students can understand.

- The past participle of regular verbs is the same as the simple past form (verb + -ed). See Appendices 4 and 5 for spelling and pronunciation rules for verbs ending in -ed.
- Irregular verbs have special past participle forms. See Appendix 6 for irregular verbs and their past participles.
- See Appendix 14 for contractions with *have*.

Common error tips help students avoid mistakes.

Do not confuse the contraction of *is* with the contraction of *has* in the present perfect.

He's **doing** research. = He **is doing** research. (He's currently doing research.)

He's **done** research. = He **has done** research. (He did research at some time in the past.)

Do not repeat *have/has* when present perfect verb phrases are connected by *and* or *or*.

He **has washed** his face and **brushed** his teeth.

The Meaning and Use section(s) offers clear and comprehensive explanations of how the target structure is used, and exercises to practice using it appropriately.

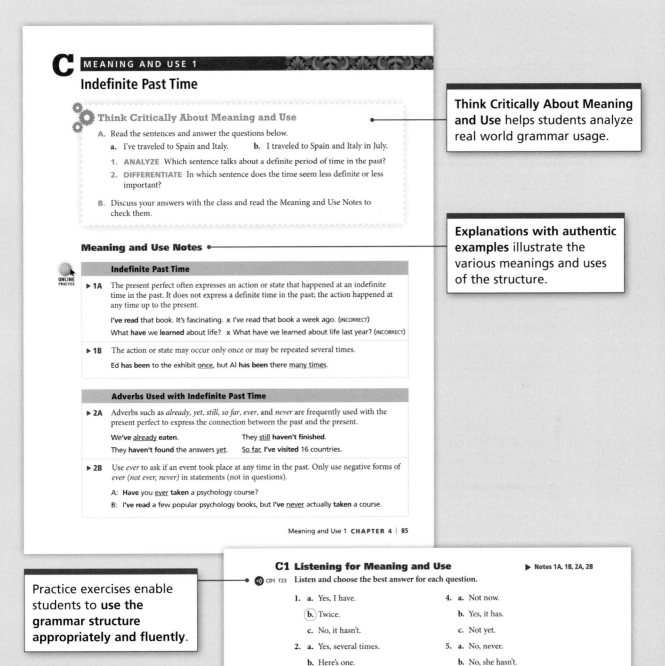

C MEANING AND USE 1

Indefinite Past Time

Think Critically About Meaning and Use

A. Read the sentences and answer the questions below.

    a. I've traveled to Spain and Italy.   b. I traveled to Spain and Italy in July.

    1. **ANALYZE** Which sentence talks about a definite period of time in the past?

    2. **DIFFERENTIATE** In which sentence does the time seem less definite or less important?

B. Discuss your answers with the class and read the Meaning and Use Notes to check them.

Think Critically About Meaning and Use helps students analyze real world grammar usage.

Meaning and Use Notes

ONLINE PRACTICE

Indefinite Past Time

▶ **1A** The present perfect often expresses an action or state that happened at an indefinite time in the past. It does not express a definite time in the past; the action happened at any time up to the present.

I've read that book. It's fascinating. x I've read that book a week ago. (INCORRECT)

What **have** we **learned** about life? x What have we learned about life last year? (INCORRECT)

▶ **1B** The action or state may occur only once or may be repeated several times.

Ed **has been** to the exhibit <u>once</u>, but Al **has been** there <u>many times</u>.

Adverbs Used with Indefinite Past Time

▶ **2A** Adverbs such as *already, yet, still, so far, ever,* and *never* are frequently used with the present perfect to express the connection between the past and the present.

We've <u>already</u> **eaten**.   They <u>still</u> **haven't finished**.

They **haven't found** the answers <u>yet</u>.   <u>So far</u>, **I've visited** 16 countries.

▶ **2B** Use *ever* to ask if an event took place at any time in the past. Only use negative forms of *ever (not ever, never)* in statements (not in questions).

A: **Have** you <u>ever</u> **taken** a psychology course?

B: **I've read** a few popular psychology books, but **I've** <u>never</u> actually **taken** a course.

Explanations with authentic examples illustrate the various meanings and uses of the structure.

Meaning and Use 1 **CHAPTER 4** | 85

C1 Listening for Meaning and Use   ▶ Notes 1A, 1B, 2A, 2B

CD1 T23   Listen and choose the best answer for each question.

Practice exercises enable students to **use the grammar structure appropriately and fluently.**

1. **a.** Yes, I have.
   b. Twice.
   c. No, it hasn't.

2. **a.** Yes, several times.
   b. Here's one.
   c. No, she hasn't.

3. **a.** No, I haven't.
   b. She's coming soon.
   c. Yes, it has.

4. **a.** Not now.
   b. Yes, it has.
   c. Not yet.

5. **a.** No, never.
   b. No, she hasn't.
   c. No, I haven't.

6. **a.** No, not yet.
   b. Everything, except the laundry.
   c. I've already done it.

Special sections appear throughout the chapters with clear explanations, authentic examples, and follow-up exercises.

Beyond the Sentence demonstrates how structures function differently in extended discourses.

Informally Speaking clarifies the differences between written and spoken language.

Beyond the Sentence

Introducing a Topic with the Simple Present

The simple present is often used in the first sentence of a paragraph to express a general statement about a topic. The sentences that follow offer more specific details and may be in the simple present or other tenses. For example:

Many people suffer from a condition called insomnia. In fact, insomnia **is becoming** the most common sleep disorder in the United States. People with insomnia **are** unable to fall asleep easily, and they **wake up** many times during the night. As a result, they always **feel** tired during the day. Their constant fatigue **can affect** their work and all aspects of their lives.

C6 Introducing a Topic with the Simple Present

A. Write five or six general statements about people in the country or city you are living in. Write about children, adults, college students, teenagers, men, women, senior citizens, and so on.

College students don't get enough sleep.
In the United States, not many people retire before they're 60.

B. Choose one of your general statements as the topic sentence of a paragraph. Write a paragraph that explains the statement in more detail.

College students don't get enough sleep. They often stay up very late. Then they sleep for only four or five hours and drag themselves to morning classes...

Vocabulary Notes

Habitual Past with *Used To* and *Would*

Used To *Used to* is a special simple past tense verb. *Used to* suggests a comparison between the past and the present. It suggests that a repeated action or state was true in the past, but is not true now, even if the present is not mentioned.

We **used to** go skating a lot. Now we go skiing.
We **didn't use to** play cards.

Used To and *Would* In affirmative statements, *would* can sometimes replace *used to* without changing the meaning. *Would* generally combines only with verbs that express actions.

When I was young, we **would** go skating a lot.
x We **would** live in China. (INCORRECT)

In a description about the past, *used to* can appear once or twice at the beginning of a paragraph, but *would* is used to provide the details in the rest of the story.

In the 1980s, I **used** to work for a big company that was far from my home. Every morning I <u>would</u> get up at 6:00 A.M. to get ready for work. I <u>would</u> leave the house by 7:00 A.M. Sometimes I <u>would</u> carpool with a neighbor...

C5 Describing the Habitual Past

Work with a partner. Put these sentences in order to form a meaningful paragraph. Discuss the use of the simple past, *used to*, and *would*.

_____ That all changed a few summers ago after we finished college and got our first jobs.

_____ In the mornings, my twin brother and I would get up early and go for hikes in the woods.

__1__ My family and I used to spend all our summers at a cottage on a lake.

_____ We didn't have a TV at the cottage, so we would spend our evenings talking and reading.

_____ We miss the lake and all the wonderful times we used to have there.

_____ Our cottage there was like our home away from home, and we loved our life there.

_____ In the afternoons, we'd meet our friends and go swimming at the lake.

_____ Every June we would leave our apartment in New York City and head for the lake.

Vocabulary Notes highlight the connection between the key vocabulary and grammatical structures.

🎧 Informally Speaking

Omitting Auxiliaries and *You*

🔊 CD1 T4 Look at the cartoon and listen to the conversation. How is each underlined form in the cartoon different from what you hear?

Are you feeling OK?

No. I have a headache. Do you have any aspirin?

Simple Present Questions In informal speech, *do* is often omitted from *Yes/No* questions with *you*. *You* is omitted only if the question is easy to understand without it.

Standard Form	What You Might Hear
Do you take the subway to work?	"You take the subway to work?"
Do you want some help?	"(You) want some help?"

Present Continuous Questions In informal speech, *are* is often omitted from *Yes/No* questions with *you*. *You* may also be omitted.

Standard Form	What You Might Hear
Are you having a good time?	"(You) having a good time?"
Are you feeling OK?	"(You) feeling OK?"

B5 Understanding Informal Speech

🔊 CD1 T5 Listen to the advertisements and write the standard form of the words you hear.

1. _Are you feeling_ tired in the morning?
2. _____ a vacation?
3. _____ car problems again?
4. _____ it yourself?
5. _____ any old clothes in your closets?
6. _____ to shop late?
7. _____ too hard?
8. _____ a house sitter?

The Writing section guides students through the process of applying grammatical knowledge to compositions.

WRITING
Write an Article for Your School's Online Newspaper

 Think Critically About Meaning and Use

A. Work with a partner. Read each situation. Choose the sentence that is the most certain.

1. The key is missing.
   a. It may be on the table.
   b. It must be on the table.
   c. It ought to be on the table.

2. A letter has just arrived.
   a. It can't be from Mary.
   b. It must not be from Mary.
   c. It might not be from Mary.

3. Thomas is doing his homework.
   a. He might finish by four o'clock.
   b. He could finish by four o'clock.
   c. He won't finish by four o'clock.

4. The answer is 25.
   a. That may not be right.
   b. That couldn't be right.
   c. That might not be right.

5. The doorbell is ringing.
   a. It has to be the mail carrier.
   b. It should be the mail carrier.
   c. It ought to be the mail carrier.

6. My car is at the service station.
   a. It won't be ready soon.
   b. It will probably be ready soon.
   c. It ought to be ready soon.

B. Discuss these questions in small groups.

1. **GENERATE** Look at sentence 1. Imagine you know for sure that the key is <u>not</u> on the table. What two modal forms could you use to replace *must be*?

2. **PREDICT** Look at sentence 6a. What might the speaker say next to support the idea?

> Integrating grammar into the writing process helps students **see the relevance of grammar to their own writing.**

Edit

Find the errors in this paragraph and corre[...]

A migraine is a severe headache that can [...] sufferers often experience symptoms such as [...] vision. However, there are other symptoms th[...] coming. You maybe sensitive to light, sound, [...] The good news is that treatment must often [...]

> Editing exercises focus students on **identifying and correcting problems** in sentence structure and usage.

Write

Imagine that you are the health editor of your school's online newspaper. Write an article discussing ways that students might stay fit while they are studying at your school. Use modals and phrasal modals of present and future possibility.

1. **BRAINSTORM** Think about all the problems that students face and the solutions that you might include. Use these categories to help you organize your ideas into three or four paragraphs.
   - **Problems:** Why might students find it difficult to stay fit while they are studying (e.g., sitting for too many hours, study/sleep habits, food)?
   - **Solutions/Advice:** What are some of the things that students might do to stay fit (e.g., exercise, eat properly, get enough sleep)?
   - **Conclusion:** What may happen if they don't follow your advice? What benefits might they experience if they follow your suggestions?

2. **WRITE A FIRST DRAFT** Before you write your first draft, read the checklist below and look at the examples on pages 146–147. Write your draft using modals of possibility.

3. **EDIT** Read your work and check it against the checklist below. Circle grammar, spelling, and punctuation errors.

DO I ...	YES
give my article a title?	☐
organize my ideas into paragraphs?	☐
use a variety of modals of possibility to speculate about the problems students may be facing now and the solutions they might consider in the near future?	☐
use adverbs such as *maybe, perhaps,* and *probably* to soften my ideas?	☐

4. **PEER REVIEW** Work with a partner to help you decide how to fix your errors and improve the content. Use the checklist above.

> Collaborating with classmates in **peer review** helps students improve their own grammar skills.

Assessment

PART 1
TEST | The Present, Past, and Future

Choose the correct word or words to complete each sentence.

1. What _____ at his corporate job?
   a. your father does
   c. does your father do
   b. do your father
   d. does your father

2. Passengers used to wait on long lines before the airlines _____ electronic check-in machines.
   a. introduce
   c. introduced
   b. used to introduce
   d. introducing

3. In what city _____ going to be?
   a. the next Olympic games will
   c. will the next Olympic games
   b. are the next Olympic games
   d. the next Olympic games are

What is expressed in each sentence? Choose the correct answer.

4. I'm living with John this semester.

> **Part Tests** allow ongoing assessment and evaluate the students' mastery of the grammar.

Teacher's Resources

Teacher's Book

- Creative techniques for presenting the grammar, along with troubleshooting tips, and suggestions for additional activities

- Answer key and audio scripts

- Includes a *Grammar Sense Online Practice* Teacher Access Code

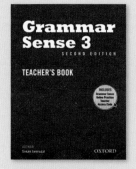

Test Generator CD-ROM

- Over 3,000 items available!

- Test-generating software allows you to customize tests for all levels of Grammar Sense

- Includes a bank of ready-made tests

Class Audio

- Audio CDs feature exercises for discriminating form, understanding meaning and use, and interpreting non-standard forms

Grammar Sense Teachers' Club site contains additional teaching resources at www.oup.com/elt/teacher/grammarsense

Grammar Sense Online Practice is an online program with all new content. It correlates with the *Grammar Sense* student books and provides additional practice.

FOR THE STUDENT

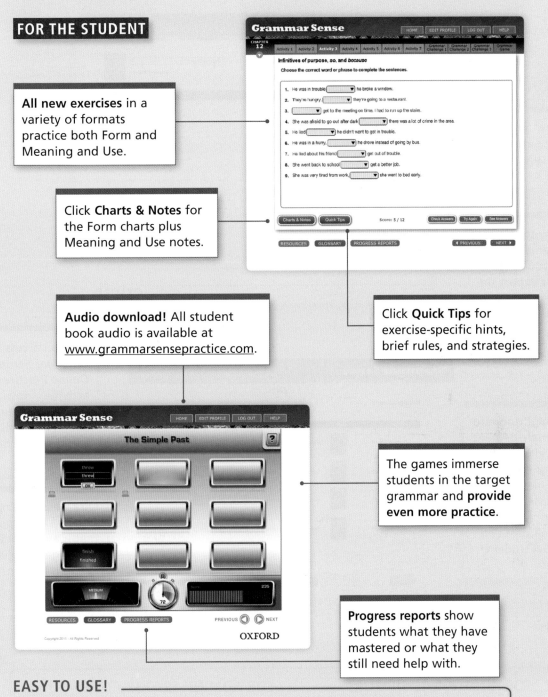

All new exercises in a variety of formats practice both Form and Meaning and Use.

Click **Charts & Notes** for the Form charts plus Meaning and Use notes.

Audio download! All student book audio is available at www.grammarsensepractice.com.

Click **Quick Tips** for exercise-specific hints, brief rules, and strategies.

The games immerse students in the target grammar and **provide even more practice**.

Progress reports show students what they have mastered or what they still need help with.

EASY TO USE!

Use the access code printed on the inside back cover of this book to register at www.grammarsensepractice.com. See the last page of the book for registration instructions.

Flexible enough for use in the classroom or easily assigned as homework.

Grammar Sense Online Practice **automatically grades** student exercises and tracks progress.

The easy-to-use online management system allows you to **review**, **print, or export** the reports you need.

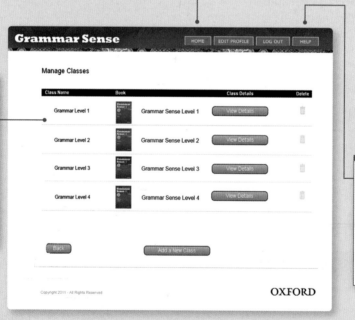

The **straightforward online management system** allows you to add or delete classes, manage your classes, plus view, print, or export all class and individual student reports.

You can **access all** *Grammar Sense Online Practice* **activities**, download the student book audio, and utilize the additional student resources.

Click Help for simple, step-by-step support that is **available in six languages**: English, Spanish, Korean, Arabic, Chinese, and Japanese.

FOR ADDITIONAL SUPPORT
Email our customer support team at grammarsensesupport@oup.com and you will receive a response within 24 hours.

FOR ADMINISTRATOR CODES
Please contact your sales representative for an Administrator Access Code. A Teacher Access Code comes with every Teacher's Book.

PART 1

1

The Present, Past, and Future

CHAPTER 1

1

The Present

3

You Snooze, You Win at Today's Workplace

A1 Before You Read

Discuss these questions.

How much sleep do you get each night? Do you usually get enough sleep? Why or why not? Do you ever take naps?

A2 Read

CD1 T2 Read this magazine article to find out how some businesses are helping their tired employees.

You Snooze, You Win at Today's Workplace

It's early afternoon and lunch is over. You're sitting at your desk and plowing through paperwork. Suddenly you're fighting to keep your eyes open. The
5 words on your computer are zooming in and out of focus, and your head is beginning to bob in all directions. A nap sounds good right about now—so does a couch or reclining armchair.

10 Well, a growing number of companies are beginning to accept the idea of sleeping on the job. No, it's not a dream. Employees are increasingly sleeping less and working longer
15 hours at the office. Some employers, therefore, are warming up to the idea that a midday nap helps increase productivity, creativity, and safety.

Some companies are now providing
20 tents in quiet areas of their offices. Each one contains a sleeping bag, a foam pad, an MP3 player, eye shades, and yes, an alarm clock. In Japan, some firms have "nightingale rooms"
25 where employees are encouraged to take "power naps," and nap salons are springing up around the globe in cities like London, Amsterdam, Tokyo, and New York.

30 Professor William Anthony, author of *The Art of Napping*, predicts that people will see the benefits of napping more and more, especially because the workplace is getting more competitive
35 and the workforce is aging.

It's no secret that most people are not getting enough sleep. The average adult needs about 500 more hours of sleep per year, based on the
40 assumption that eight hours of sleep per night is normal. Two out of three people get less than eight hours of sleep a night during the work week, according to a recent study by a well-
45 known sleep foundation. Forty percent say they're so tired that it interferes with their daily activities.

Professor Anthony rarely misses a nap. He says that companies should permit
50 napping during breaks. "Workers are sleepy, and when they're sleepy on the job, they're not productive."

Nevertheless, at most companies, napping on the job is not yet
55 acceptable. In fact, it sometimes leads to dismissal. Still, that doesn't stop some nappers, according to Professor Anthony. He found that "they're napping in their cars, in the bathroom,
60 or in vacant rooms. Others are trying to hide their naps in their cubicles. They're putting the phone to their ear, or pretending to write or read something."

Adapted from *The Christian Science Monitor*

bob: to move repeatedly up and down
cubicle: a small enclosed area
dismissal: telling an employee that he or she is fired
plow through: to force one's way through

productivity: the amount of work you can do in a certain time
snooze: to nap
warm up to: to begin to like

A3 After You Read

Write *T* for true or *F* for false for each statement.

__T__ 1. Tired workers produce fewer products.

__T__ 2. Some employers provide special napping areas.

__F__ 3. People need to sleep a total of five hundred hours a year.

__F__ 4. One study shows that most adults get eight hours of sleep per night.

__T__ 5. Most companies do not encourage napping.

__F__ 6. Employees only nap at the office.

B | FORM

The Simple Present and the Present Continuous

A. Look back at the article on page 4 and complete the tasks below.

1. **IDENTIFY** Look at the underlined verb forms. Draw one line under six more simple present verb forms. Draw two lines under six more present continuous verb forms.

2. **COMPARE AND CONTRAST** Find a negative statement in the simple present and the present continuous. Describe the differences between them.

3. **GENERATE** Change the following sentences to *Yes/No* questions. What changes do you have to make?
   a. The average adult sleeps six hours a night.
   b. Americans are sleeping less.

B. Discuss your answers with the class and read the Form charts to check them.

▶ The Simple Present

ONLINE
PRACTICE

AFFIRMATIVE STATEMENTS			
SUBJECT		**VERB OR VERB + -S/-ES**	
I		**work**	
She	usually	**works**	on weekends.
They		**work**	

NEGATIVE STATEMENTS			
SUBJECT	**DO/DOES + NOT**	**VERB**	
I	**don't**		
She	**doesn't**	**sleep**	enough.
They	**don't**		

▶ The Present Continuous

AFFIRMATIVE STATEMENTS		
SUBJECT + *BE*	**VERB + *ING***	
I**'m**		
She**'s**	**working**	right now.
They**'re**		

NEGATIVE STATEMENTS		
SUBJECT + *BE + NOT*	**VERB + *ING***	
I**'m not**		
She**'s not** / She **isn't**	sleeping	well.
They**'re not** / They **aren't**		

▶ The Simple Present

YES/NO QUESTIONS

DO/DOES	SUBJECT	VERB	
Do	you		
Does	she	**work**	on weekends?
Do	they		

SHORT ANSWERS

AFFIRMATIVE		NEGATIVE	
	I **do**.		I **don't**.
Yes,	she **does**.	**No,**	she **doesn't**.
	they **do**.		they **don't**.

INFORMATION QUESTIONS

WH-WORD	DO/DOES	SUBJECT	VERB	
Why	**do**	you	**work**	late?
Where	**does**	she	**live**?	
What	**do**	they	**think**?	

WH-WORD	VERB + -S/-ES	
Who	**works**	late?
What	**happens**	now?

▶ The Present Continuous

YES/NO QUESTIONS

BE	SUBJECT	VERB + ING	
Are	you		
Is	she	**working**	now?
Are	they		

SHORT ANSWERS

AFFIRMATIVE		NEGATIVE	
	I **am**.		I'**m not**.
Yes,	she **is**.	**No,**	she**'s not**. / she **isn't**.
	they **are**.		they**'re not**. / they **aren't**.

INFORMATION QUESTIONS

WH-WORD	BE	SUBJECT	VERB + ING	
Why	**are**	you	**working**	late?
Where	**is**	she	**living**?	
What	**are**	they	**thinking**?	

WH-WORD	IS	VERB + -S/-ES	
Who	**is**	**working**	late?
What		**happening?**	

The Simple Present

- Affirmative statements can use *do* or *does*, but only for emphasis.

    You're wrong. I **do** like her.

- See Appendices 1 and 2 for spelling and pronunciation rules for verbs ending in -s and -es.

- See Appendix 14 for contractions with *do*.

(Continued on page 8)

The Present Continuous

- To combine present continuous sentences with *and*, use the subject and *am/is/are* only once.

    You**'re sitting** at your desk and **going** through paperwork.

- *Is not /are not* can be used instead of the contracted form for emphasis in negative short answers.

    No, he **is not**.   No, they **are not**.

- Stative verbs (verbs that do not express actions) are not usually used with the present continuous. The simple present is used instead.

    I **own** a house.

    x I'm owning a house. (INCORRECT)

- See Appendix 3 for spelling rules for verbs ending in *-ing*.

- See Appendix 14 for contractions with *be*.

B1 Listening for Form

CD1 T3   Lee is a student who is living away from home. Listen to the questions that his family asks him over the phone. Choose the best response for each question.

1. **a.** Yes, I am.
    b. Yes, I do.
    c. Yes, it is.

2. **a.** Yes, I do.
    b. Yes, they are.
    c. Yes, I am.

3. **a.** Yes, I have.
    b. Yes, I do.
    c. Yes, I am.

4. **a.** Yes, she is.
    b. Yes, we are.
    c. Yes, they are.

5. **a.** Yes, I do.
    b. Yes, I am.
    c. Yes, I have.

6. **a.** No, it doesn't.
    b. No, I don't.
    c. No, they don't.

7. **a.** Yes, he does.
    b. No, he's not.
    c. Yes, he is.

8. **a.** No, it doesn't.
    b. Yes, it is.
    c. Yes, there are.

B2 Working on Verb Forms

Complete the verb chart. Add *-s/-es* and *-ing* where necessary and make spelling changes.

	BASE FORM	SIMPLE PRESENT	PRESENT CONTINUOUS
1.	sleep	sleep/sleeps	sleeping
2.	open		
3.	fix		
4.	stop		
5.	wake		
6.	say		
7.	rest		
8.	dry		

B3 Working on Present Continuous Statements and Questions

Complete these conversations with the words in parentheses and the present continuous. Use contractions when possible.

Conversation 1: A child walks into the house on a rainy day.

Parent: Please take off your boots.

Child: __I'm not wearing boots.__ (I/not/wear/boots) _____
             1   2

(I/wear/shoes) Do I need to take them off, too?

Conversation 2: Amy sees Sam at the vending machine.

Amy: _____ (you/buy/a soda?)
                 1

Sam: No, _____ (I/not/get/anything)
                    2

Amy: _____ (what/you/do?)
                 3

Sam: _____ (I/try/to get back/my money)
                 4

Conversation 3: Ann is taking everything out of the desk drawer.

Bill: _____ (what/you/do?)
                 1

Ann: _____ (I/look for/a pencil)
                 2

Bill: _____ (why/you/make/such a mess?)
                 3

There are pencils in the kitchen.

B4 Working on Simple Present Statements and Questions

A. Work with a partner. The statements below are false. Make each one true by changing it to a negative statement. Then write a true statement using the word in parentheses instead of the underlined word.

1. Water freezes at 0° <u>Fahrenheit</u>. (centigrade)

   Water doesn't freeze at 0° Fahrenheit. It freezes at 0° centigrade.

2. Earth revolves around the <u>moon</u>. (sun)

   _____

3. Palm trees grow in <u>cold</u> climates. (warm)

   _____

4. Bees live in <u>ponds</u>. (hives)

   _____

5. The sun rises in the <u>north</u>. (east)

   _____

6. Penguins live in <u>the desert</u>. (the Antarctic)

   _____

7. Flowers bloom in the <u>winter</u>. (summer)

   _____

8. Spiders have <u>six</u> legs. (eight)

   _____

B. Make up a question related to each fact above. Then take turns asking and answering the questions with your partner.

A: *What temperature does water freeze at?*
B: *Water freezes at 0° centigrade.*

OR

A: *Does water freeze at 0° Fahrenheit?*
B: *No, it doesn't. It freezes at 0° centigrade.*

Informally Speaking

Omitting Auxiliaries and *You*

CD1 T4 Look at the cartoon and listen to the conversation. How is each underlined form in the cartoon different from what you hear?

Simple Present Questions In informal speech, *do* is often omitted from *Yes/No* questions with *you*. *You* is omitted only if the question is easy to understand without it.

Standard Form	What You Might Hear
Do you take the subway to work?	"You take the subway to work?"
Do you want some help?	"(You) want some help?"

Present Continuous Questions In informal speech, *are* is often omitted from *Yes/No* questions with *you*. *You* may also be omitted.

Standard Form	What You Might Hear
Are you having a good time?	"(You) having a good time?"
Are you feeling OK?	"(You) feeling OK?"

B5 Understanding Informal Speech

CD1 T5 Listen to the advertisements and write the standard form of the words you hear.

1. _Are you feeling_ tired in the morning?

2. _____ a vacation?

3. _____ car problems again?

4. _____ it yourself?

5. _____ any old clothes in your closets?

6. _____ to shop late?

7. _____ too hard?

8. _____ a house sitter?

Contrasting the Simple Present and the Present Continuous

Think Critically About Meaning and Use

A. Look at the pictures and answer the questions below.

1. **ANALYZE** In which picture is the conversation about something that is in progress at the moment (happening now)?

2. **ANALYZE** In which picture is the conversation about a repeated action or routine?

B. Discuss your answers with the class and read the Meaning and Use Notes to check them.

Meaning and Use Notes

ONLINE PRACTICE

	Using the Simple Present
▶ **1A**	The simple present is used to talk about repeated activities, such as habits, routines, or scheduled events. Adverbs of frequency and time expressions (such as *usually* and *every hour*) often occur with the simple present. **Routines:** I <u>usually</u> **drink** two cups of coffee in the morning. **Schedules:** The bus **comes** <u>every hour</u>.
▶ **1B**	The simple present can also describe factual information, such as general truths or definitions. **General Truths:** Some babies **don't sleep** at night. **Definitions:** A recliner **is** a comfortable chair that **leans** back.

Using the Present Continuous

▶ **2A** In contrast to the simple present, the present continuous is used for activities in progress at the exact moment of speaking. Adverbs and time expressions such as *now*, *right now*, and *at this moment* often occur with the present continuous.

> **Activities in Progress at This Exact Moment**
>
> I'm **drinking** a cup of coffee right now.   It's 3:00 A.M.! Why **isn't** the baby **sleeping**?

▶ **2B** The present continuous can also express the extended present—an activity in progress over a period of time that includes the present, such as *this week* and *these days*. The activity may be ongoing or may stop and start repeatedly during the time. The extended present is often used to express changing situations.

> **Activities in Progress over a Period of Time (Extended Present)**
>
> I'm **drinking** a lot of coffee this week.   The baby **is sleeping** better these days.
>
> **Changing Situations**
>
> The bus **is coming** later and later this semester.

Permanent Situations vs. Temporary Situations

▶ **3** Sometimes the simple present and present continuous are close in meaning, but not exactly the same. If a situation is permanent or habitual, choose the simple present. If a situation is new or temporary, choose the present continuous.

Simple Present (Permanent or Habitual)	Present Continuous (New or Temporary)
We **live** on Eddy Street. We moved there ten years ago.	We'**re living** on Eddy Street. We just moved in.
I **stay** here every summer.	I'm **staying** here for the summer.

Expressing Complaints vs. Expressing Facts

▶ **4** Present continuous sentences with adverbs of frequency that mean "all of the time" (such as *always*, *constantly*, *continually*, and *forever*) often express complaints. Sentences in the simple present are more neutral or factual—they do not generally express complaints.

Simple Present (Neutral Attitude)	Present Continuous (Expressing Complaints)
They <u>always</u> **call** me early Sunday morning.	They **are** <u>always</u> **calling** me early Sunday morning. I hate when they wake me up.
My brother <u>constantly</u> **plays** computer games.	My brother **is** <u>constantly</u> **playing** computer games. He needs to study more.

C1 Listening for Meaning and Use

▶ Notes 1A, 1B, 2A, 2B

 CD1 T6   Listen and choose the best answer for each question.

1. **a.** I'm relaxing.
   b. I read books.
   c. Listen to music.

2. **a.** Two kids.
   b. Yes, I do.
   c. No, it's true.

3. **a.** I'm resting.
   b. Working at night.
   c. I'm a sales associate.

4. **a.** Yes, she does.
   b. I know.
   c. He leaves.

5. **a.** No, just in the morning.
   b. Because I like it.
   c. Yes, I am.

6. **a.** I mean it.
   b. A short period of sleep.
   c. Yes, he's mean.

7. **a.** Yes, he does.
   b. No, he isn't.
   c. To Jonah.

8. **a.** Yes, it's hard.
   b. Because of my work.
   c. Yes, I am.

C2 Contrasting Activities in Progress with Routine Activities

▶ Notes 1A, 2A

A. Work in small groups. Use the present continuous to discuss what is going on in the picture. What are the people doing? What is happening?

B. Work on your own. Use the present continuous to describe what you are doing right now. Then use the simple present to write sentences that describe your daily routines at work, school, and home.

ACTIVITIES IN PROGRESS AT THE MOMENT	DAILY ROUTINES
I'm sitting in class.	I take the bus every morning at 7:00.
I'm listening to the English teacher.	I go to English class on Mondays and Wednesdays.

C3 Describing Activities in the Extended Present ▶ Note 2B

Write five sentences describing activities that you are involved in. Use the present continuous and *this year*, *these days*, or *this semester*. Then discuss your answers in small groups. Were any of your answers the same?

I'm learning to ski this year. I'm also running a lot.

C4 Contrasting Permanent and Temporary Situations ▶ Note 3

Work in small groups. Match each sentence on the left with the sentence on the right that provides the best context. Discuss your choices.

___c__ **1.** Tomek lives on Dryden Road.　　**a.** He usually wears jeans and a T-shirt.

_____ **2.** Peter is living on Dryden Road.　　**b.** He has worked there since 1990.

_____ **3.** Alex wears a tie to school.　　**c.** He has lived there for a long time.

_____ **4.** Matt is wearing a tie to school.　　**d.** He started the job a few days ago.

_____ **5.** Luis works at the bank.　　**e.** He's a very formal dresser.

_____ **6.** Andrew is working at the bank.　　**f.** He just moved there a few weeks ago.

C5 Expressing Complaints

▶ Note 4

 Work in small groups. Complain about the behavior of people you know, politicians, or other famous people. Use *always*, *constantly*, *continually*, and *forever* with the present continuous.

My brother is always watching sports on TV.
My neighbor is constantly playing loud music.
The governor is continually losing his temper in public.
She is forever talking on the phone.

Beyond the Sentence

Introducing a Topic with the Simple Present

The simple present is often used in the first sentence of a paragraph to express a general statement about a topic. The sentences that follow offer more specific details and may be in the simple present or other tenses. For example:

Many people **suffer** from a condition called insomnia. In fact, insomnia **is becoming** the most common sleep disorder in the United States. People with insomnia **are** unable to fall asleep easily, and they **wake up** many times during the night. As a result, they always **feel** tired during the day. Their constant fatigue **can affect** their work and all aspects of their lives.

C6 Introducing a Topic with the Simple Present

A. Write five or six general statements about people in the country or city you are living in. Write about children, adults, college students, teenagers, men, women, senior citizens, and so on.

College students don't get enough sleep.
In the United States, not many people retire before they're 60.

B. Choose one of your general statements as the topic sentence of a paragraph. Write a paragraph that explains the statement in more detail.

College students don't get enough sleep. They often stay up very late. Then they sleep for only four or five hours and drag themselves to morning classes...

D

MEANING AND USE 2

Verbs with Stative Meanings vs. Verbs with Active Meanings

Think Critically About Meaning and Use

A. Read the sentences and answer the questions below.

a. I have a new computer at work.
b. I usually use it quite a bit.
c. It's more powerful than my co-workers' computers.

d. I do research on my computer.
e. I feel good about my job.

1. **CATEGORIZE** Which sentences express actions?

2. **CATEGORIZE** Which sentences express states or conditions?

B. Discuss your answers with the class and read the Meaning and Use Notes to check them.

Meaning and Use Notes

ONLINE PRACTICE

States and Conditions

▶ 1 Stative verbs do not express actions. They express states and conditions. They commonly occur in the simple present.

> My roommate's name **is** Peter. He**'s** tall and **has** brown hair. He **likes** sports cars and loud music.

Below are some common stative verbs.

Descriptions and Measurements

- be, appear, look, seem, look like, resemble
- sound, sound like
- cost, measure, weigh

Possession and Relationships

- have, possess, own
- belong, owe, depend on
- consist of, contain, include

Knowledge and Beliefs

- believe, guess, hope, feel (= think), know, think, doubt
- remember, forget, recognize, notice
- mean, understand, realize, suppose
- agree, disagree

Emotions and Attitudes

- dislike, fear, hate, like, love, despise
- care, mind
- need, prefer, want, desire, appreciate

Senses and Sensations

- hear, see, smell, taste
- ache, burn, feel, hurt, itch, sting

(Continued on page 18)

Distinguishing Verbs with Stative and Active Meanings

▶ **2A**   Some verbs with stative meanings also have active meanings and can express activities in the present continuous.

Simple Present (Stative)	Present Continuous (Active)
I **think** this pie is delicious. (belief)	We**'re thinking** about moving. (mental activity)
It **weighs** a lot. (measurement)	I**'m weighing** it on the scale. (physical activity)

▶ **2B**   When *have* means "possess" it expresses a state and can be used in the simple present, but not in the present continuous. When *have* means "experience," "eat," or "drink," it has an active meaning and can be used in the continuous.

Simple Present (Stative)	Present Continuous (Active)
Peter **has** two cars.	**Are** you **having** any problems? (experience)
We **have** a computer at home.	I**'m having** dinner with Sue. (eating)

▶ **2C**   Sense verbs with stative meanings express involuntary (uncontrolled) states in the simple present. In the present continuous, *smell* and *taste* have active meanings that express voluntary actions.

Simple Present (Stative)	Present Continuous (Active)
This soup **tastes** great.	I**'m tasting** the soup to see if it's too hot.
I **smell** something awful.	I**'m smelling** each flower to find my favorite.

Expressing Physical Sensations

▶ **3**   Verbs that express physical sensations can occur in the simple present or the present continuous without changing the meaning.

Simple Present (Stative)	Present Continuous (Active)
My stomach **hurts** and I **feel** sick.	My stomach **is hurting** and I**'m feeling** sick.

Using *Be* + Adjective for Behavior

▶ **4**   Adjectives such as *good*, *bad*, *rude*, and *foolish* describe behavior. To express typical behavior, use these adjectives with the simple present of *be*. If the behavior is temporary or not typical, however, use them with the present continuous of *be*.

Simple Present (Typical Behavior)	Present Continuous (Not Typical Behavior)
My kids **are good**. They always behave well in restaurants.	My kids **are being good** today! They usually don't behave well in restaurants.

D1 Listening for Meaning and Use ▶ Note 1

 CD1 T7　Listen to each situation. Is the speaker talking about a state or condition or about an activity? Check (✓) the correct column.

	STATE OR CONDITION	ACTIVITY
1.	✓	
2.		
3.		
4.		
5.		
6.		

D2 Making Critical Remarks with Stative Verbs ▶ Note 1

Work with a partner. You are in a bad mood. Respond to your friend's comments and questions with a critical remark. Use the words in the box. Then switch roles.

VERBS		ADJECTIVES	
be	look	awful	loud
cost	seem	cheap	small
feel	smell	crowded	strong
like	sound	expensive	terrible

1. **Your Friend:** Let's go into this store. There's a big sale.

   You: *I don't want to. It looks crowded.*

2. I think I'll buy some of this cologne. I really like it.

3. I like this shirt. The fabric is nice.

4. I love these shoes. How do they look on me?

5. Listen to this song. Doesn't it sound great?

6. I need a new tennis racket. This one looks like a good buy.

D3 Choosing the Simple Present or the Present Continuous

▶ Notes 1, 2A–2C

Work with a partner. Complete these conversations with the words in parentheses and the simple present or the present continuous. Use contractions when possible. Then practice the conversations.

Conversation 1

A: What course ___are you taking___ (you/take) with Professor Hale?
     1

B: Psychology 101.

A: _____ (it/be) a good course?
              2

B: Well, that _____ (depend on) my mood.
                       3

   I _____ (guess) it _____ (be) OK, but
          4   5

   I _____ (have) trouble with our latest assignment.
          6

Conversation 2

A: Excuse me. I _____ (hope) I _____ (not/interrupt),
                          1   2

   but I _____ (need) some help with my car.
              3

B: What _____ (seem) to be the problem?
                  4

A: I _____ (smell) something bad. Maybe it's the engine.
              5

Conversation 3

A: How often _____ (you/dream)? I _____
                        1   2

   (not/dream) very often at all these days.

B: That's not true. Everyone _____ (have) dreams every night.
                                          3

   You probably _____ (not/remember) most of your dreams.
                        4

Conversation 4

A: What _____ (you/do)?
                  1

B: I _____ (smell) the milk. I _____ (think)
              2   3

   it's spoiled.

A: Well, how _____ (it/smell)?
                        4

B: It _____ (seem) fine.
                5

D4 Describing Physical Sensations

▶ Note 3

Work with a partner. Use the simple present or the present continuous with these verbs to describe your symptoms for each of the problems below.

feel   hurt   ache   tingle   itch   burn

1. You have a sore throat.

   A: *What's wrong?*
   B: *My throat feels sore.* OR *My throat is feeling sore.*

2. You have a headache.

3. You have something in your eye.

4. You have a sprained ankle.

5. You have a stomachache.

6. You have a rash on your arm.

D5 Describing Behavior

▶ Note 4

A. Work in small groups. Build as many meaningful sentences as possible. Use an item from each column. Punctuate your sentences correctly. Discuss why some combinations are not appropriate.

The birds are quiet. The birds are being quiet.

the birds the flowers the children	are are being	quiet sick rude purple

B. Imagine you have heard these comments at work. Explain the use of *is* or *is being* by giving more details about each situation.

1. Walter is being so polite.

   He is usually very rude. OR
   He often insults people.

2. Marta is very helpful.

3. The company is being generous.

4. The employees are being so quiet.

5. Mr. Johnson is unfair.

6. My boss is being difficult.

7. My neighbor is being unfriendly.

Informally Speaking

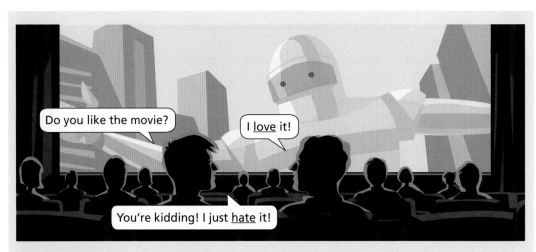

Expressing Emotions in the Continuous

CD1 T8 Look at the cartoon and listen to the conversation. How is each underlined form in the cartoon different from what you hear?

In informal speech, some verbs may be used in the continuous form but keep their stative meaning. This is especially common with verbs of emotion such as *love*, *hate*, and *like*. Using the continuous shows a more intense or emotional situation. Adverbs such as *just* or *really* and special emphatic intonation are often used as well.

Standard Form	What You Might Hear
I **love** this novel.	"I'm just loving this novel!"
I **hate** this movie.	"I'm really hating this movie!"
I **like** it here.	"I'm really liking it here!"

D6 Understanding Informal Speech

CD1 T9 Listen and write the standard form of the words you hear.

1. _I like_ _____ my apartment more and more each day!

2. _____ this new television show!

3. _____ the beautiful weather!

4. _____ this trip!

5. _____ this movie!

6. _____ my new job.

D7 Writing Descriptions

▶ Notes 1–4

Follow these steps to write a summary about a favorite character in a book, movie, or TV show.

1. In small groups, brainstorm a list of three or four of your favorite books, movies, or TV shows. Discuss your favorite character in each and explain why you like him or her.

2. Choose one character that you have discussed. Write a description in the simple present about this person. Tell what happens to him or her, how the person looks, feels, and so on, using verbs with stative meaning where appropriate.

The "Wizard of Oz" tells the story of Dorothy. She is a young girl and she lives on a farm in Kansas. After a big storm, she lands in Oz. Dorothy feels frightened at first, but soon after…

The Wizard of Oz

⚙ Think Critically About Meaning and Use

A. Read each sentence and answer the questions that follow with one of these choices: *Yes, No, Probably, Probably not,* or *It's not clear.*

1. I'm writing a book.

    a. Is the speaker finished with the book yet? _No._____

    b. Did the speaker start writing the book a few days ago? _____

    c. Is the speaker writing at the moment of speaking? _____

2. The bus is stopping.

    a. Is the bus speeding up? _____

    b. Is the driver's foot on the brake? _____

    c. Are the passengers getting off the bus? _____

3. My sister works at the Computing Center.

    a. Is she working right now? _____

    b. Did she get the job yesterday? _____

    c. Does she work full-time? _____

4. I'm sleeping much better this week.

    a. Is the speaker sleeping right now? _____

    b. Did the speaker sleep well last week? _____

    c. Will the speaker sleep well next week? _____

5. I'm taking a French course right now.

    a. Is the speaker in the French class right now? _____

    b. Has the course begun? _____

    c. Is the course over? _____

6. I watch the news during breakfast.

    a. Is the speaker watching the news? _____

    b. Is the speaker eating breakfast? _____

    c. Will the speaker watch the news during breakfast tomorrow?

    _____

B. Discuss these questions in small groups.

1. **COMPARE AND CONTRAST** What is the difference in meaning between sentence 1 and the statement "I write books"?

2. **PREDICT** Look at sentences 1, 3, and 5. What do you think the speakers will say next? (Use the simple present and present continuous in your answers.)

Edit

Find the errors in these paragraphs and correct them.

It's mid-afternoon at a busy law firm. The telephones ~~is~~ *are* ringing, voice mail piles up, and faxes are arriving. But what many of the lawyers are doing? They take naps at their desks! As more and more busy professionals works from morning until night, many are sleep in their offices for just 15 or 20 minutes during the afternoon. And they are not embarrassed about it at all. It becomes a new trend, according to a recent survey on napping.

Some people sleeps in their chairs, while some are preferring the floor or couches. Everyone agrees that a little nap help them get through their very long workday. Meanwhile, many experts are asking "What means this new trend?" It's simple, according to the most experienced nappers. They are do what people in other cultures and climates do every day. And they are pleased that napping finally gets more common in the workplace.

Write

Imagine that you are a new student at a college or university. Update your profile page on a social networking site. Use the simple present and present continuous.

1. **BRAINSTORM** Think about all the things you can say about your new life. Use these categories to help you organize your ideas into paragraphs.
   - **Self and School:** who you are; where you're going to school; what courses you're taking; how you feel about your new situation
   - **Living Situation:** where you are living; your roommates, if any; how you like it
   - **Routines, Free-Time:** study habits; typical weekday; free-time activities

2. **WRITE A FIRST DRAFT** Before you write your first draft, read the checklist below and look at the sentences you wrote for tasks C2 (part B) and C3 on page 15. Write your draft using the simple present and present continuous.

3. **EDIT** Read your work and check it against the checklist below. Circle grammar, spelling, and punctuation errors.

DO I...	YES
organize my ideas into paragraphs?	☐
use the simple present for facts, habits, schedules, and routines?	☐
use the present continuous for activities in progress now and in the extended present?	☐
use stative verbs in the simple present to describe states and conditions?	☐
use contractions to make my writing sound more friendly and natural?	☐

4. **PEER REVIEW** Work with a partner to help you decide how to fix your errors and improve the content. Use the checklist above.

5. **REWRITE YOUR DRAFT** Using the comments from your partner, write a final draft.

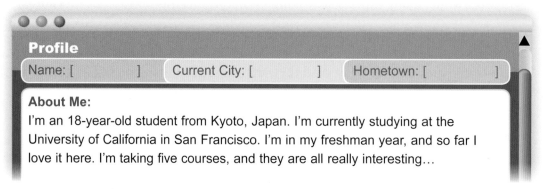

Profile

Name: [   ] Current City: [   ] Hometown: [   ]

About Me:
I'm an 18-year-old student from Kyoto, Japan. I'm currently studying at the University of California in San Francisco. I'm in my freshman year, and so far I love it here. I'm taking five courses, and they are all really interesting...

CHAPTER

2

The Past

A Night to Remember

A1 Before You Read

 Discuss these questions.

What are some important news events from your lifetime? Do you remember where you were when they occurred? What were you doing at that particular time?

A2 Read

 CD1 T10 **Read this book excerpt to find out what was happening when the *Titanic* hit an iceberg.**

A NIGHT TO REMEMBER

It was April 14, 1912, the fifth night of the *Titanic*'s first trip. At almost 11:40 P.M., Frederick Fleet and Reginald Lee, two of the ship's "lookouts," were on duty.
5   They were watching for icebergs when Fleet suddenly saw something directly ahead. At first it was small, but every second it grew larger and closer. Quickly, Fleet banged the bell three times to warn
10 of danger ahead. He also lifted the phone and rang the bridge.
    "What did you see?" asked a calm voice at the other end.
    "Iceberg right ahead," replied Fleet.
15   "Thank you," said the voice calmly.
    At this moment George Thomas Rowe, one of the ship's officers, was standing watch. Suddenly, he felt a curious motion break the steady rhythm of the
20 engines. He glanced forward—and stared again. He thought he saw a ship before he realized it was an iceberg. The next instant it was gone.
    Meanwhile, down below in the first
25 class dining room, four other members of the *Titanic*'s crew were sitting around one of the tables. They were doing what off-

duty stewards often did—they were gossiping about the passengers. Then,
30 while they were talking, a grinding vibration seemed to come from deep inside the ship. It was not much, but it was enough to break their conversation and rattle the silver that was on the
35 breakfast tables for the next morning.
    In the kitchen, Chief Night Baker Walter Belford was making rolls for the following day. When the jolt came, it impressed Belford strongly. Perhaps this
40 was because a pan of fresh rolls clattered off the top of the oven and scattered about the floor.

Most of the *Titanic*'s passengers were in bed when the strange vibration
45 occurred. But a few were still up. As usual, they were in the first class smoking room. Around one table, some men were enjoying a final cigar. At another table, the ship's younger passengers were enjoying a lively
50 game of bridge. While they were playing and laughing, they suddenly felt that grinding vibration. Some people ran out onto the deck. When they got there, they saw the iceberg. It was scraping the side of
55 the ship. In another moment it faded into the darkness. The excitement, too, soon disappeared. The group went back inside, and the bridge game continued.

Down in Boiler Room No. 6, Fireman
60 Fred Barrett was talking to an assistant engineer when the warning bell rang. A quick shout of warning—an ear-splitting crash—and the whole side of the ship seemed to collapse. The sea rushed in and
65 swirled around the pipes and valves. Before the watertight door slammed down, the two men leaped through the doorway into Boiler Room No. 5. Unfortunately, they found things almost
70 as bad there...

Adapted from *A Night to Remember*

clatter: to make a series of knocking noises
grinding: rubbing together harshly
jolt: a sudden forceful shake
stand watch: to be on duty on a ship

steward: a man who helps passengers and serves meals
vibration: a shaking movement

A3 After You Read

Choose the answer that best completes each sentence.

1. Crew members were watching for _____.

   a. seagulls   **b.** rain   **c.** icebergs

2. The dining room stewards were _____.

   a. cleaning up   **b.** sleeping   **c.** talking

3. The baker was making _____.

   a. pies   **b.** rolls   **c.** cakes

4. _____ of the passengers were in bed.

   a. All   **b.** Most   **c.** None

5. Some of the passengers _____.

   a. saw the iceberg   **b.** warned the captain   **c.** were worried

6. Water poured into _____ first.

   a. the kitchen   **b.** the boiler rooms   **c.** the captain's quarters

B FORM

The Simple Past, the Past Continuous, and Time Clauses

Think Critically About Form

A. Look back at the book excerpt on page 28 and complete the tasks below.

1. **IDENTIFY** Two examples of the simple past are underlined. Find three regular and three irregular simple past verb forms.

2. **RECOGNIZE** An example of the past continuous is circled. Find six more examples. Sort your examples into singular and plural.

3. **ANALYZE** Find examples of clauses beginning with *when*, *while*, and *before*. Do these clauses come before or after the main clause they are connected to?

B. Discuss your answers with the class and read the Form charts to check them.

▶ The Simple Past

AFFIRMATIVE STATEMENTS

SUBJECT	VERB + -D/-ED OR IRREGULAR FORM	
I	**worked**	that night.
He	**felt**	scared.
They	**traveled**	by ship.

NEGATIVE STATEMENTS

SUBJECT	DID + NOT	VERB	
I		**work**	that night.
He	**didn't**	**feel**	scared.
They		**travel**	by ship.

▶ The Past Continuous

AFFIRMATIVE STATEMENTS

SUBJECT	WAS/WERE	VERB + -ING	
I	**was**	**working**	that night.
He	**was**	**feeling**	scared.
They	**were**	**traveling**	by ship.

NEGATIVE STATEMENTS

SUBJECT	WAS/WERE + NOT	VERB + -ING	
I	**wasn't**	**working**	that night.
He	**wasn't**	**feeling**	scared.
They	**weren't**	**traveling**	by ship.

▶ The Simple Past

YES/NO QUESTIONS

DID	SUBJECT	VERB	
Did	you	**work**	that night?
	he	**feel**	scared?
	they	**travel**	by ship?

SHORT ANSWERS

AFFIRMATIVE			NEGATIVE		
Yes,	I		No,	I	
	he	**did**.		he	**didn't**.
	they			they	

INFORMATION QUESTIONS

WH-WORD	DID	SUBJECT	VERB	
When		you	**work**	there?
Why	did	he	**feel**	scared?
Where		they	**travel**	to?

WH-WORD		VERB + -D/-ED OR IRREGULAR FORM	
Who		**worked**	late?
What		**happened**?	

▶ The Past Continuous

YES/NO QUESTIONS

WAS/WERE	SUBJECT	VERB + -ING	
Were	you	**working**	that night?
Was	he	**feeling**	scared?
Were	they	**traveling**	by ship?

SHORT ANSWERS

AFFIRMATIVE			NEGATIVE		
Yes,	I	**was**.	No,	I	**wasn't**.
	he	**was**.		he	**wasn't**.
	they	**were**.		they	**weren't**.

INFORMATION QUESTIONS

WH-WORD	WAS/WERE	SUBJECT	VERB + -ING	
When	were	you	**working**	there?
Why	was	he	**feeling**	scared?
Where	were	they	**traveling**	to?

WH-WORD	WAS		VERB + -ING	
Who			**working**	late?
What	was		**happening**?	

The Simple Past
- See Appendices 4 and 5 for spelling and pronunciation rules for verbs ending in -ed.
- See Appendix 6 for irregular verbs and their simple past forms and Appendix 14 for contractions with *did*.

The Past Continuous
- Stative verbs are not usually used in the past continuous. Use the simple past instead.

   I **owned** a house.   x I was owning a house. (INCORRECT)

- See Appendix 3 for spelling rules for verbs ending in -*ing* and Appendix 14 for contractions with *was/were*.

(Continued on page 32)

▶ The Simple Past and The Past Continuous in Time Clauses

TIME CLAUSE	MAIN CLAUSE
While the crew **was working**,	the passengers **were sleeping**.
Before the noise **interrupted** them,	they **were playing** cards.

MAIN CLAUSE	TIME CLAUSE
The passengers **were sleeping**	while the crew was **working**.
Water **flooded** the ship	after it **struck** the iceberg.

- Time clauses begin with time words such as *while, when, before,* or *after*. They are dependent clauses and cannot stand alone as complete sentences. They must be attached to independent main clauses to complete their meaning.
- A time clause can come before or after the main clause. The meaning is the same. If the time clause comes first, it is followed by a comma.

B1 Listening for Form

CD1 T11   Listen to this news report and write the verb forms you hear.

Where ___were___ you when the lights _____ out this morning? That's
           1   2
the question everyone is asking today. Early this morning, a construction crew

_____ on 33rd Street while people across the city _____ to work. At
     3   4
8:29 A.M., a simple mistake by the construction crew _____ a blackout that
                                                            5
_____ power to almost a million people.
     6
    The blackout _____ airports to send incoming flights elsewhere. But
                       7
according to one report, a jet liner _____ just when the power in the control
                                          8
tower _____. After the jet _____ contact with the tower, the pilot
          9   10
_____ the plane himself with no problems.
     11
    The mayor _____ a state of emergency. Fortunately, no major accidents
                    12
or injuries _____, and the power _____ after six hours and twenty minutes,
               13   14
at 2:49 this afternoon.

B2 Building Simple Past and Past Continuous Sentences

Build as many meaningful sentences as possible. Use an item from each column, or from the second and third columns only. Punctuate your sentences correctly.

When did you buy a computer?

when did what did what were did	who what you	paid cash studying this morning buy a computer happened last night do when the bell rang go online yesterday

B3 Identifying Dependent and Independent Clauses

Check (✓) the examples that can stand alone as full sentences. Correct the punctuation of those sentences.

_____ ✓ 1. ̶h̶e̶ He was standing on the deck of the Titanic.

_____ 2. while the stewards were talking

_____ ✓ 3. something vibrated inside the ship

_____ 4. before midnight

_____ ✓ 5. the iceberg hit the ship .

_____ ✓ 6. some passengers were getting ready for bed

_____ 7. after the incident

_____ ✓ 8. a group was still playing bridge

_____ 9. while others were wandering about

_____ 10. after the men escaped

B4 Combining Sentences with Time Clauses

 Work with a partner. Combine the sentences with the time word in parentheses to form as many sentences with time clauses as possible.

1. I went home. I finished my work. (when)

   When I went home, I finished my work. OR *I finished my work when I went home.*
   When I finished my work, I went home. OR *I went home when I finished my work.*

2. He was reading. He was listening to music. (while)

3. He went to law school. He studied hard. (after)

4. She fell asleep. The doorbell rang. (before)

5. The fire started. We were sleeping. (when)

6. The TV show started. They went to bed. (before)

7. The phone was ringing. They were cooking dinner. (while)

8. The package arrived. She called the post office. (before)

B5 Asking and Answering Questions with Time Clauses

 Work with a partner. Take turns asking and answering the questions.

1. What were you doing…
   before this class started?
   when the teacher walked in?
   when the class ended yesterday?
   while you were eating breakfast?

   A: What were you doing before this class started?
   B: I was talking to my friends.

2. Where were you living…
   when you were a child?
   while you were in high school?
   before you came to this town/city?

3. What were you thinking about…
   when you went to sleep last night?
   when you woke up this morning?
   while you were coming to class?
   before you walked in the door?

Contrasting the Simple Past and the Past Continuous

Think Critically About Meaning and Use

A. Read the sentences and answer the questions below.

1a. The warning bell rang.   **2a.** The bakers cleaned up.
1b. The warning bell was ringing.   **2b.** The bakers were cleaning up.

ANALYZE Which sentences describe a completed event? an unfinished event?

B. Discuss your answers with the class and read the Meaning and Use Notes to check them.

Meaning and Use Notes

ONLINE
PRACTICE

The Simple Past for Completed Past Situations

▶ **1** The simple past describes an action or state that started and finished at a definite time in the past. The action or state can last for a short or long period of time, occur in the recent or distant past, and happen once or repeatedly.

Short Period of Time	**Long Period of Time**
The rain **lasted** for 30 seconds.	The rain **lasted** for many days.

Recent Past	**Distant Past**
She **was** very sick last week.	She **was** very sick last year.

Happened Once	**Happened Repeatedly**
She **arrived** late last week.	She always **arrived** late.

The Past Continuous for In-Progress Past Situations

▶ **2A** The past continuous expresses an activity in progress at an exact moment in the past. The activity began before the specific point in time and might also have continued after that time.

Activities in Progress at an Exact Moment

He **was getting ready** for bed at 11:40 P.M. He still wasn't ready ten minutes later.

(Continued on page 36)

> **▶ 2B** The past continuous may also express an activity in progress over an extended period of time in the past. The activity may have been ongoing or may have stopped and started repeatedly.

> **Activities in Progress over an Extended Period of Time**
>
> They **were working** on the project for two years.

Completed vs. In-Progress Past Situations

> **▶ 3A** The past continuous and the simple past can be similar in meaning, but not exactly the same. To describe a situation as completed, choose the simple past. To describe the same situation in progress, choose the past continuous.

> | **Simple Past (Completed)** | **Past Continuous (In Progress)** |
> | --- | --- |
> | I **lived** on Eddy Street in 1986. | I **was living** on Eddy Street while I was in school. |

> **▶ 3B** The simple past implies the completion of an event. The past continuous often emphasizes the activity or process. The past continuous activity may or may not have been completed.

> | **Simple Present (Stative)** | **Present Continuous (Active)** |
> | --- | --- |
> | He **wrote** a letter in the library and **mailed** it on his way home. (He finished the letter.) | He **was writing** a letter in the library when the lights went out. (We don't know if he finished the letter.) |

The Past Continuous for Background Information

> **▶ 4** The past continuous often appears at the beginning of a narrative to describe background activities. It can express several background activities happening at the same time as the main event. The main event is in the simple past.

> It **was raining** hard outside. I **was sleeping** and my roommate **was taking** a shower. At exactly 7:00 A.M., there <u>was</u> a huge clap of thunder. I <u>jumped up</u> as the house <u>shook</u> violently…

C1 Listening for Meaning and Use

▶ Notes 3A, 3B

 CD1 T12 Listen to descriptions of these activities. Check (✓) whether the activity is completed at the end of the description or may continue after the end of the description.

	ACTIVITY	COMPLETED	MAY CONTINUE
1.	writing a book		✓
2.	eating dinner		
3.	painting his kitchen		
4.	baking a cake		
5.	writing a letter		

C2 Describing Activities in Progress in the Past

▶ Notes 2A, 2B

Look at the picture and describe the different activities that were happening yesterday afternoon at the public library. Use the past continuous.

Many people were waiting in line at the reference desk.
One man was chasing his child around the book carts.

C3 Contrasting In-Progress and Completed Past Situations

▶ Notes 3A, 3B

Read this interview by a dorm advisor who is investigating a false fire alarm in a college dorm. Choose the simple past or past continuous forms that best complete the conversation.

Advisor: What ((did you notice)/ were you noticing) last night?
                                         1

Student: It was after dinner and I was in the student lounge. Four male students

(played / were playing) a game at a table. Three others
       2

(studied / were studying) together on the couches. A female student
       3

(read / was reading) a newspaper in the corner. I (did / was doing) a
     4   5

crossword puzzle. At eight o'clock, I (heard / was hearing) two of my friends
                                            6

in the hall. They (told / were telling) jokes, so I (went / was going) into the
               7   8

hall to talk to them. On the way back to my seat, I (stopped / was stopping)
                                                          9

to talk to the guys at the table. Suddenly we (heard / were hearing) the fire
                                                    10

alarm go off. We all (jumped / were jumping) up and (ran / were running)
                            11   12

out of the lounge. We (didn't smell / weren't smelling) smoke and we
                            13

(didn't see / weren't seeing) anything suspicious, but just to be safe we
        14

(went / were going) down the emergency stairs and (got / were getting) out
     15   16

of the building as fast as we could.

C4 Describing Background Activities

▶ Note 4

A. Write two past continuous sentences that describe activities that were happening at the same time as each of the simple past events.

1. My phone rang at 7:00 A.M.

   I was sleeping. My roommate was taking a shower.

2. We watched the evening news at 6:30.

3. Lightning struck a huge tree in our yard this afternoon.

4. I stopped at the supermarket on my way home from work.

5. My computer crashed last night.

6. The fire alarm rang during class.

B. Write a paragraph about an item in part A. Begin with background information in the past continuous. Then use the simple past to describe the main event.

   At 7:00 A.M., I was sleeping and my roommate was taking a shower. Suddenly, the phone rang. I jumped out of bed, picked up the phone, and said sleepily, "Hello?...

Vocabulary Notes

Habitual Past with *Used To* and *Would*

Used To *Used to* is a special simple past tense verb. *Used to* suggests a comparison between the past and the present. It suggests that a repeated action or state was true in the past, but is not true now, even if the present is not mentioned.

> We **used to go** skating a lot. Now we go skiing.

> We **didn't use to play** cards.

Used To* and *Would In affirmative statements, *would* can sometimes replace *used to* without changing the meaning. *Would* generally combines only with verbs that express actions.

> When I was young, we **would go** skating a lot.

> x We would live in China. (INCORRECT)

In a description about the past, *used to* can appear once or twice at the beginning of a paragraph, but *would* is used to provide the details in the rest of the story.

> In the 1980s, I **used to** work for a big company that was far from my home. Every morning I <u>would</u> get up at 6:00 A.M. to get ready for work. I <u>would</u> leave the house by 7:00 A.M. Sometimes I <u>would</u> carpool with a neighbor…

C5 Describing the Habitual Past

Work with a partner. Put these sentences in order to form a meaningful paragraph. Discuss the use of the simple past, *used to*, and *would*.

_____ That all changed a few summers ago after we finished college and got our first jobs.

_____ In the mornings, my twin brother and I would get up early and go for hikes in the woods.

__1__ My family and I used to spend all our summers at a cottage on a lake.

_____ We didn't have a TV at the cottage, so we would spend our evenings talking and reading.

_____ We miss the lake and all the wonderful times we used to have there.

_____ Our cottage there was like our home away from home, and we loved our life there.

_____ In the afternoons, we'd meet our friends and go swimming at the lake.

_____ Every June we would leave our apartment in New York City and head for the lake.

Beyond the Sentence

Using the Simple Past in Discourse

Simple Present Introductions to Descriptions of the Past General statements in the simple present can often introduce simple past descriptions. The simple past gives specific details about the simple present statement.

> Voice mail systems **are** often frustrating. Last week, I <u>tried</u> to call an airline company. First, I <u>listened</u> to a menu with six different choices. Then I…

Time Expressions with the Simple Past In a simple past description, a time expression such as *last weekend* often appears in the description, but not in every sentence. Each sentence relates to this time until a new expression appears. Often a change of time expression (for example, *now*) signals a change in tense.

> I **called** Jill <u>last weekend</u>, and she **was** sick with the flu. She **sounded** terrible so we **didn't talk** very long. I **spoke** to her again <u>this morning</u>, and she **was** much better. She**'s** back at work <u>now</u>, and everything **seems** fine.

C6 Using the Simple Past in Discourse

A. Read each simple present introductory statement. Then write a sentence in the simple past that adds a detail. Tell when the particular experience happened.

1. You can't depend on the weather. <u>Last year, we ran into terrible fog during our trip through Austria.</u>

2. I still remember my childhood. _____

_____

3. I don't like long lines. _____

_____

B. Write a short paragraph. Choose one of the items in part A. Pay attention to your use of time expressions for keeping or changing sentences.

> *You can't depend on the weather. Last year, we ran into terrible fog during our trip through Austria. It was our first time in the Austrian countryside, and we barely saw anything as we rode from town to town. The whole countryside was under a dense fog. We were very disappointed so we…*

The Simple Past and the Past Continuous in Time Clauses

Think Critically About Meaning and Use

A. Read the sentences and answer the questions below.

a. They were talking about the passengers when they suddenly felt the vibration.
b. Some people were sleeping while others were playing cards.
c. When the bell rang, he yelled to his assistant.

1. ANALYZE Which sentence shows that one completed event happened after another completed event?

2. ANALYZE Which sentence shows that one event interrupted another event?

3. ANALYZE Which sentence shows that two events were happening at the same time?

B. Discuss your answers with the class and read the Meaning and Use Notes to check them.

Meaning and Use Notes

ONLINE
PRACTICE

Sequential Events	
▶ **1A**	Past time clauses describe the time relationship of two past events and show the order of those events. Sentences with two simple past clauses can show that one completed event happened after the other. *Before*, *after*, or *when* introduces the time clause.

Simple Past (1st Event)	**Simple Past (2nd Event)**
I wrote the letter	**before I heard the news**.
After I heard the news,	I wrote the letter.
When I heard the news,	I wrote the letter.

▶ **1B**	Sometimes a sentence with a when or after time clause expresses a cause-and-effect relationship. The first event causes the second event.

Cause (1st Event)	**Effect (2nd Event)**
When the power went out,	the room got completely dark.
After the power went out,	the room got completely dark.

(Continued on page 42)

Interrupted Events

▶ **2A**   Sentences with one simple past and one past continuous clause typically show that a simple past event interrupted a past continuous event.

He **was studying** for exams when the lights **went out**.

OR

Before the lights **went out**, he **was studying** for exams.

▶ **2B**   Both *while* and *when* introduce a past continuous clause that means "during the time."

Past Continuous (1st Event)	Simple Past (2nd Event)
While I was dancing,	I lost my necklace.
When I was dancing,	I lost my necklace.

▶ **2C**   *When* can also introduce a simple past clause that means "at the time," but *while* cannot.

Past Continuous (1st Event)	Simple Past (2nd Event)
I was dancing	when I lost my necklace.
x I was dancing	while I lost my necklace. (INCORRECT)

Simultaneous Events

▶ **3**   Sentences with two past continuous clauses typically show that two activities were happening at the same time. Both *while* and *when* can introduce the time clause.

Past Continuous	Past Continuous
They were laughing	while they were playing cards.
They were laughing	when they were playing cards.

D1 Listening for Meaning and Use

▶ Notes 1A, 1B, 2A, 2B

CD1 T13 Listen to the two events in each statement and choose the event that happened or started first.

1. **a.** I went home.

    b. I opened the mail.

2. **a.** I played tennis.

    b. I took a shower.

3. **a.** The phone rang.

    b. I was fixing the bathroom sink.

4. **a.** She came home.

    b. It started to rain.

5. **a.** I was waiting for John.

    b. I saw Erica.

6. **a.** The water ran out.

    b. I opened the drain.

7. **a.** I called the operator.

    b. She connected me with Bogotá.

8. **a.** I shouted.

    b. She turned around.

D2 Using Past Time Clauses

▶ Notes 1A, 1B, 2A–C, 3

Work in groups. Read this account of the Johnstown Flood of 1889. Make notes about what happened. Then make up as many sentences as you can with *while, when, before,* and *after* time clauses. Include sequential, interrupted, and simultaneous events in your sentences.

Before the water crashed into Johnstown, the train engineer tried to warn people.

It was May 31, 1889. It was raining, and the waters of a nearby lake were rising. The South Fork Dam was sagging. A few minutes after 3:00 P.M. that day, the dam collapsed and a 40-foot wall of water headed toward Johnstown, 14 miles away. A train engineer outside of the town tried to warn people that the flood was coming. He sped down the track and blew his train whistle loudly. This time, he didn't toot the whistle three times in his usual friendly way. Instead, he made the whistle wail in a way that survivors remembered years later.

The water crashed into Johnstown at a very high speed. Some people called it a tidal wave. The flood destroyed everything in its path. It wiped out villages, bridges, and freight trains. Many people had no time to leave their homes. They ran to the upper floors of their houses and they climbed onto their roofs. The force of the water lifted some houses and knocked them into each other. Other people were luckier. They were able to escape to the hills right above Johnstown.

After the tragedy, people from around the world donated 4 million dollars to help Johnstown, and more than 200 photographers came to record the story. It was the first big international news event. Johnstown survived two more major floods in 1936 and 1977.

D3 Relating Events with *Before* and *After*

▶ Notes 1A, 1B, 2A

A. Describe the changes in each pair of pictures. Use *before* and *after*.

Situation 1: Her grades came in the mail.

Before her grades came in the mail, she was worried. After her grades came in the mail...

Situation 2: He tripped and fell.

Situation 3: Their parents came home.

B. Write a short story about one of the pairs of pictures. Use time clauses in your story to describe what happened before and after.

Elena was standing at the window, waiting for the mail. Her exam grades were late...

D4 Understanding Cause and Effect

▶ Note 1B

Work with a partner. Read each pair of sentences and label the cause and the effect. Then combine the sentences, using *when* or *after* to express the cause. Discuss why more than one answer is possible in some sentences.

1. **a.** The roads became icy. ___*effect*___

   b. The temperature dropped below freezing. ___*cause*___

   When the temperature dropped below freezing, the roads became icy.

2. **a.** They had to call for help. _____

   b. They ran out of gas. _____

   _____

3. **a.** The lightning struck. _____

   b. The lights went out. _____

   _____

4. **a.** They painted their house bright pink. _____

   b. The neighbors refused to talk to them. _____

   _____

5. **a.** He went on a strict diet. _____

   b. His best suit didn't fit anymore. _____

   _____

6. **a.** Her arm started to itch. _____

   b. A mosquito bit her. _____

   _____

7. **a.** The doorbell rang. _____

   b. He answered the door. _____

   _____

8. **a.** She found the lost jewelry. _____

   b. She got a reward. _____

   _____

D5 Talking About Interrupted Activities

Notes 2A–2C

A. Complete this email message by writing sentences with *when* and *while* time clauses about the events in parentheses. Use the simple past or the past continuous.

From: tsmith@email.com

To: miguel@email.com

Subject: A Very Bad Day

Hi Miguel!

You wouldn't believe what a terrible day I had! _While I was trying to sleep,_
[1]
the cat jumped on my chest (I try to sleep / the cat jumps on my chest).

So I got up to let him go out, but _____ (I go down the stairs /
[2]
I trip on a shoe). By this time, I was fully awake even though it was just 5:15 in the morning. So I

decided to make breakfast. Would you believe that _____
[3]
(I make coffee / I spill the whole can of coffee on the floor)? I tried to calm down, eat my breakfast,

and get ready for school. But _____ (I take a shower / the
[4]
phone rings). So I got out of the shower to answer it, but _____
[5]
(I step out of the shower / I slip on the wet floor). I finally answered the phone, and it was an old friend

who drives me crazy! He asked to come and visit me. I told him he couldn't come. _____

_____ (I try to explain / he gets mad and hangs up).
[6]

Well, I got to school all right. The most important thing that I had to do today was to write a paper for

my economics class. Well, guess what? _____ (I write the paper
[7]
/ the computer system goes down). I had to go to class without my paper. Then _____

_____ (I ride the elevator to class / it gets stuck). I was 45 minutes late, so I
[8]
missed most of my class. Fortunately, my professor has a sense of humor.

Thanks for reading all of this nonsense! How was your day?

 B. Work with a partner. Can you remember a day when something unexpected happened? Take turns telling each other what happened. Use time clauses and the simple past or the past continuous.

| **CHAPTER 2** The Past

Think Critically About Meaning and Use

A. Read each sentence and the statement that follows. Write *T* if the statement is true, *F* if it is false, or *?* if you do not have enough information to decide.

1. Before the storm arrived, the weather stations were warning us about it.

   ___F___ The storm began before the weather stations warned us.

2. The children were building a snowman while it was snowing.

   _____ They finished the snowman.

3. He wrote a book about the *Titanic*.

   _____ He completed the book.

4. We lost our power when a tree came down.

   _____ A tree came down after we lost our power.

5. He was listening to the news while she was sleeping.

   _____ She fell asleep before the news started.

B. Discuss these questions in small groups.

1. **COMPARE AND CONTRAST** What happens to the meaning of sentence 2 if we change *were building* to *built*?

2. **GENERATE** How could you expand sentence 3 to make it more informative? (Make 3 different sentences using *while*, *before*, and *when*.)

Edit

Some of these sentences have errors. Find the errors and correct them.

1. While he was taking a shower, ~~when~~ someone called.

2. After he fell asleep, he was reading a book. *bef or*

3. Were you having your own car in college? *did* *have*

4. He didn't go to class yesterday.

5. Oh, no! I was dropping my earring. I can't find it. *dropped*

6. I dialed again, after I heard the dial tone.

Write

Write a narrative essay about a memorable experience from your childhood. Use the simple past, the past continuous, and the habitual past with *used to* and *would*.

1. **BRAINSTORM** Think about all the things you might want to include when writing about the experience. Use these categories to help you organize your ideas into paragraphs.
   - **What your life was like around the time of the experience:** how old you were; things you used to do or think; places and/or people that were important to you
   - **The memorable experience:** background activities that were happening when the experience began; the series of events that made up the memorable experience
   - **Why the experience was important to you:** what you learned; how it affected you

2. **WRITE A FIRST DRAFT** Before you write your first draft, read the checklist below and look at the examples in tasks C3, C4, and C5 on pages 38–39.

3. **EDIT** Read your work and check it against the checklist below. Circle grammar, spelling, and punctuation errors.

DO I ...	YES
organize my ideas into paragraphs?	☐
use *used to* and *would* to talk about the habitual past?	☐
use the past continuous for background activities and activities in progress?	☐
use the simple past for main events and completed states and situations?	☐
use past time expressions and past time clauses?	☐

4. **PEER REVIEW** Work with a partner to help you decide how to fix your errors and improve the content. Use the checklist above.

5. **REWRITE YOUR DRAFT** Using the comments from your partner, write a final draft.

> One of my most memorable experiences of my childhood happened when I was ten. At the time, I was a very lonely child. I used to come straight home from school, and after dinner, I'd go to my room and spend the evening by myself...

C H A P T E R

3

Future Forms

A GRAMMAR IN DISCOURSE

Trend Forecasters Predict Future

A1 Before You Read

Discuss these questions.

Do you think people can predict the future? Make some predictions that you think will come true in the next ten or twenty years.

A2 Read

CD1 T14 Read this newspaper article to find out what two experts predict for the future.

Trend Forecasters Predict Future

Want to know what the future holds for us? Ask a trend forecaster. Businesses pay them millions of dollars for help in predicting what products people are going to
5 buy. Here are a few predictions made by two well-known trend forecasters, Faith Popcorn and Gerald Celente.

According to Faith Popcorn:
• "Knowledge chips" planted in our brains will
10 enable us to speak French instantly, repair the TV, learn golf, or whatever.
• We will become more sensitive to issues related to food and consumer products. Vegan-friendly retailing is going to increase
15 dramatically, and most of us will be buying products like cruelty-free, animal-friendly vegan shoes and accessories or clothing and home furnishings made from eco-friendly fibers grown without pesticides and other chemicals.
20 • To make sure our foods are safe, we'll all own one of the "newly reliable portable food testers."

Faith Popcorn

According to Gerald Celente:
• Health, fitness, and nutrition are going to be key. People are going to do more to take care of
25 themselves.
• People will spend more on chemical-free food as their fear of contaminated meat, vegetables, and fish increases.
• Shopping malls will no longer exist.

Gerald Celente

30 • Technology will make it possible for people to test load a virtual washing machine or refrigerator in a virtual appliance department.

• Food, oil, and energy prices will continue to skyrocket, so more people will see the

35 importance of becoming self-sufficient. Many homeowners will be growing their own food, equipping their homes with solar, hydro, and wind technologies, and generating their own energy.

40 • We're also going to see a revolution in energy. It may be as big as the discovery of fire or the invention of the wheel. Advances in physics will lead to exciting new forms of energy.

---

contaminated: unclean; unfit for use
key: very important
reliable: dependable
self-sufficient: needing no outside help to satisfy one's basic needs

skyrocket: (prices) rise dramatically
trend: a current style or fashion; what people generally seem to be doing
vegan: not eating or using animal-derived products

A3 After You Read

Choose the products and trends that will become more popular according to the trend forecasters.

(1.) chemical-free foods

2. electric cars

3. robot housekeepers

4. vegan shoes

5. videophones

6. eco-friendly fibers

7. energy-independent homes

8. safe cities

9. new kinds of energy

10. larger and larger malls

11. do-it-yourself surgery

12. portable food-testers

The Future Continuous and Review of Future Forms

Think Critically About Form

A. Look back at the article on page 50 and complete the tasks below.

1. **IDENTIFY** Examples of three different future forms are underlined. Find all the other examples of these future forms and sort them into categories:
   am/is/are + *going to* + verb
   will + verb
   will be + verb + *-ing*

2. **GENERATE** Do you know any other tenses that can be used to express the future?

B. Discuss your answers with the class and read the Form charts to check them.

▶ The Future Continuous

ONLINE
PRACTICE

AFFIRMATIVE STATEMENTS				
SUBJECT	*WILL*	*BE*	VERB + *-ING*	
I				
She	will	be	coming	later.
They				

NEGATIVE STATEMENTS					
SUBJECT	*WILL*	*NOT*	*BE*	VERB + *-ING*	
I					
She	will	not	be	coming	later.
They					

YES/NO QUESTIONS				
WILL	SUBJECT	*BE*	VERB + *-ING*	
	you			
Will	she	be	coming	later?
	they			

SHORT ANSWERS						
YES	SUBJECT	*WILL*		*NO*	SUBJECT	*WON'T*
	I				I	
Yes,	she	will.		No,	she	won't.
	they				they	

INFORMATION QUESTIONS					
WH- WORD	*WILL*	SUBJECT	*BE*	VERB + *-ING*	
When	will	you	be	**coming**?	
Where		they		**working**	tomorrow?

WH- WORD	*WILL*		*BE*	VERB + *-ING*	
Who	will		be	**coming**	later?
What				**happening**	year?

- The future continuous has the same form with every subject.
- The future continuous has two auxiliary verbs: *will* and *be*. Only *will* forms contractions.
- Verbs with stative meanings are not usually used with the future continuous.

  x I'll be knowing the answer later. (INCORRECT)

- See Appendix 3 for spelling rules for verbs ending in *-ing*.
- See Appendix 14 for contractions with *will*.

▶ Review of Future Forms

THE FUTURE WITH *BE GOING TO*
AM/IS/ARE + *GOING TO* + VERB
It**'s going to rain** tonight.
It**'s not going to rain** tonight.
Is it **going to rain** tonight?
Yes, it **is**. / **No**, it **isn't**.
When is it **going to rain**?

THE FUTURE WITH *WILL*
WILL + VERB
I'll finish this soon.
I **won't finish** this soon.
Will you **finish** this soon?
Yes, I **will**. / **No**, I **won't**.
When will you **finish**?

THE PRESENT CONTINUOUS AS FUTURE
AM/IS/ARE + VERB + *-ING*
She**'s leaving** in a few minutes.
She**'s not leaving** in a few minutes.
Is she **leaving** in a few minutes?
Yes, she **is**. / **No**, she **isn't**.
When are you **leaving**?

THE SIMPLE PRESENT AS FUTURE
SIMPLE PRESENT VERB FORM
The store **opens** at ten tomorrow.
The store **doesn't open** until ten tomorrow.
Does the store **open** at ten tomorrow?
Yes, it **does**. / **No**, it **doesn't**.
What time **does** the store **open** tomorrow?

(Continued on page 54)

- All future forms can occur in the main clause of sentences with future time clauses.
- Future time clauses begin with a time word such as *when*, *before*, or *after*.
- In most sentences expressing future time, the time clause uses the simple present. Only the main clause uses a future form.

  <u>After</u> you **get** home, I**'m leaving** for work.

  I**'ll** probably **leave** for work <u>when</u> you **get** home.

B1 Listening for Form

CD1 T15   **Listen to each situation. Choose the future form that you hear.**

1. a. I call
   b. I'll call
   c. I'll be calling
   d. I'm calling

2. a. It won't be raining
   b. It won't rain
   c. It's not going to rain
   d. It's not raining

3. a. The movie starts
   b. The movie will start
   c. The movie will be starting
   d. The movie is starting

4. a. We'll cruise
   b. We're cruising
   c. We'll be cruising
   d. We're going to cruise

5. a. We'll be leaving
   b. We're going to leave
   c. We're leaving
   d. We'll leave

6. a. They're sending
   b. They'll send
   c. They'll be sending
   d. They're going to send

7. a. John will arrive
   b. John will be arriving
   c. John is going to arrive
   d. John is arriving

8. a. Do you go skiing
   b. Are you going to go skiing
   c. Will you be going skiing
   d. Are you going skiing

B2 Working on the Future Continuous

Write five sentences that tell why Abdul can't go out with his friends this week.
Use Abdul's calendar to explain what he will be doing.

Abdul will be studying for a history exam. He'll also be...

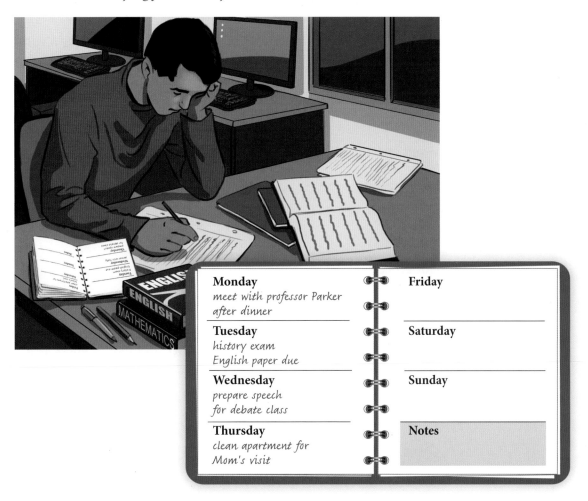

Monday		Friday
meet with professor Parker after dinner		
Tuesday		**Saturday**
history exam English paper due		
Wednesday		**Sunday**
prepare speech for debate class		
Thursday		Notes
clean apartment for Mom's visit		

B3 Building Sentences Using Future Forms

Build as many meaningful sentences as possible. Use an item from each column, or
from the first and third columns only. Use contractions when possible and punctuate
your sentences correctly.

I'll (I will) leave tomorrow.

I who her family	is going to will will be am	leaving soon leave tomorrow

B4 Asking *When* Questions About the Future

Work with a partner. Take turns asking and answering questions with *when*. Use the phrases below and *be going to*, the present continuous as future, or the future continuous. Use future time words in your answers.

1. take a vacation

   A: *When are you going to take / are you taking / will you be taking a vacation?*
   B: *This summer.*

2. get a medical checkup

3. take the day off

4. clean your apartment

5. finish your work

6. go out to dinner

7. do your laundry

8. shop for groceries

B5 Working on the Simple Present as Future

A. Read this fall semester schedule from an American university. Use the simple present as future and the verbs *begin*, *start*, *last*, and *end* to make as many sentences as possible about the schedule.

Classes start on September 1.

University Fall Semester Schedule

September 1	First day of classes
October 12–15	Fall vacation
November 22–25	Thanksgiving break
December 6	Last day of classes
December 13–20	Final exams

B. Work with a partner. Write a current school schedule like the one in part A. Take turns saying simple present sentences to talk about the future events on your schedule.

B6 Working on Future Time Clauses

Work with a partner. Combine the sentences with the time word in parentheses to form as many sentences with future time clauses as possible. Use the simple present in the time clause and *will* or *be going to* in the main clause. Are any combinations illogical?

1. He takes a shower.
    He gets out of bed. (after)

    After he gets out of bed, he'll take a shower.
    After he gets out of bed, he's going to take a shower.
    He'll take a shower after he gets out of bed.
    He's going to take a shower after he gets out of bed.

    ILLOGICAL:
    After he takes a shower, he'll get out of bed.
    After he takes a shower, he's going to get out of bed.

2. I go shopping.
    I call you. (before)

3. The mail arrives.
    I eat breakfast. (after)

4. He falls asleep.
    He reads the newspaper. (when)

5. He sets the table.
    He cooks dinner. (before)

6. I go home.
    I clean my house. (when)

Contrasting *Will* and the Future Continuous

Think Critically About Meaning and Use

A. Read the sentences and answer the questions below.

1a. Don't worry. I'll pick up the kids after work.
1b. I'll be picking up the kids after work. Then I'll be going straight home.
2a. Don't call Bob at six. He'll probably be eating dinner then.
2b. Don't call Bob at six. He'll probably eat dinner then.

1. **ANALYZE** Compare 1a and 1b. Which one describes a plan? Which one expresses a promise?

2. **ANALYZE** Compare 2a and 2b. Which one refers to an activity in progress? Which one refers to the beginning of an activity?

B. Discuss your answers with the class and read the Meaning and Use Notes to check them.

Meaning and Use Notes

ONLINE
PRACTICE

Future Activities in Progress

▶ **1** The future continuous expresses an activity in progress at a specific time in the future. Like all other continuous forms, the future continuous makes you think of a situation as ongoing.

At this time tomorrow, **I'll be leaving** for Hawaii.

I'll be staying in Hawaii for three weeks.

Promises and Requests vs. Plans and Expectations

▶ **2A** Especially in the first person, *will* and the future continuous express different meanings. A sentence with *will* can be used to make a promise. However, the same sentence in the future continuous typically expresses a plan or expectation.

Future with *Will* (a Promise)	Future Continuous (a Plan or Expectation)
I'll **finish** this tomorrow.	I'll **be finishing** this tomorrow.

> **2B** A question with *will* can be used to make a request. However, the same question in the future continuous asks about a plan or expectation. This question may lead to a request in a more indirect and polite way.

Future with *Will* **(a Request)**	**Future Continuous** **(a Question About a Plan)**
A: **Will** you **stop** at the post office tomorrow to send this package?	A: **Will** you **be stopping** at the post office tomorrow?
B: Sure.	B: Yes, I will.
	A: Could you send this package?

C1 Listening for Meaning and Use ▶ Notes 1, 2A, 2B

CD1 T16 Listen to each situation. Choose the sentence that most appropriately follows what you hear.

1. **a.** So hurry up. She'll be coming at 8:00.

   b. So hurry up. She'll come at 8:00.

2. **a.** Will you open it for me?

   b. Will you be opening it for me?

3. **a.** I won't be baking a cake today.

   b. I won't bake a cake.

4. **a.** I'll email it to you by 9:00 A.M. tomorrow.

   b. I'll be emailing it to you by 9:00 A.M. tomorrow.

5. **a.** We'll be getting back to you as soon as possible.

   b. We'll get back to you as soon as possible.

6. **a.** Will you be getting some more from the supply room?

   b. Will you get some more from the supply room, please?

7. **a.** Will you go past the bus stop?

   b. Will you be going past the bus stop?

8. **a.** … she'll be getting married.

   b. … she'll get married.

C2 Expressing Promises, Plans, and Expectations ▶ Notes 1, 2A, 2B

Work with a partner. For each situation, finish writing the conversation using the future with *will* or the future continuous. Then act out your conversations.

1. **Student A:** You are the parent. You are going away for the weekend. You are nervous about leaving your teenage son or daughter alone. Discuss your concerns with him or her.

    Student B: You are the teenager. Reassure your parent.

    Parent: I hope you'll be home by 11:00.

    Teenager: I promise I won't break any rules. Anyway, I won't be going out much. I'll be studying for my exams tonight.

    Parent: When will you be... ?

2. **Student A:** You are the employee. You need to leave early because of a family problem. Make promises about your work.

    Student B: You are the boss. Your employee has a family problem and needs to leave work early. You are concerned about your employee's problem, but the project needs to get done.

    Employee: Could I leave early today? I need to help my mother.

    Boss: Will you be able to finish your work?

    Employee: I promise I'll...

C3 Using Direct and Indirect Requests ▶ Note 2B

A. Work with a partner. Write a conversation for each situation. Use *will* to make a direct request.

1. You want to borrow your friend's math notes.

    A: Will you please lend me your math notes?
    B: Sure. No problem.

2. You want your friend to drive you to school.

3. You would like to use your brother's car.

4. Your friend is going to buy concert tickets and you would like one, too.

B. Work with the same partner. Write another conversation for each situation in part A. Use the future continuous to make an indirect request that asks about a plan. Then respond to the indirect request.

A: Will you be using your math notes this afternoon?
B: No. Do you want to borrow them?
A: Yes, I do. Thanks.

Contrasting *Be Going To,* the Present Continuous as Future, and the Simple Present as Future

 Think Critically About Meaning and Use

A. Read the sentences and answer the questions below.

    a. <u>I'm going to exercise during my lunch hour every day.</u>
    b. <u>Classes start on September 1.</u>
    c. I'm tired. <u>I'm not working tonight.</u>

Think about the meanings of the underlined sentences in each context.

    1. EVALUATE Which two sentences describe a plan that may or may not actually happen?

    2. EVALUATE Which sentence describes a scheduled event that is unlikely to change?

B. Discuss your answers with the class and read the Meaning and Use Notes to check them.

Meaning and Use Notes

ONLINE PRACTICE

Expressing Plans or Intentions

▶ **1A** Both *be going to* and the present continuous as future are used to talk about a planned event or future intention. A future time expression is stated or implied with the present continuous.

Future with *Be Going To*

He**'s not going to take** any classes this summer. He**'s going to work** full-time.

Present Continuous as Future

He**'s not taking** any classes this summer. He**'s working** full-time.

(Continued on page 62)

▶ 1B The meanings of *be going to* and the present continuous as future are sometimes similar, but not exactly the same. With *be going to*, the speaker may not have an exact plan. With the present continuous as future, the plan is often more definite.

Future with *Be Going To*

I**'m going to leave** my job (someday). I'm just so unhappy.

Present Continuous as Future

I**'m leaving** my job (next week). I've been unhappy for too long.

Expressing Scheduled Events

▶ 2A The simple present as future is used for scheduled events that usually cannot be changed. It is common in more formal contexts.

Simple Present as Future

Printed Program: The conference **starts** on Tuesday evening and **ends** on Saturday afternoon.

Trip Itinerary: The flight **leaves** Chicago at 10:02 and **arrives** in Palm Beach at 12:36.

Announcement: Our new branch office **opens** this Monday at the Cedar Mall.

▶ 2B When talking about scheduled events, the simple present, the present continuous, or *be going to* can express the same meaning. However, the simple present as future is more likely to imply that the schedule is beyond the control of the speaker.

Present Continuous as Future and Future with *Be Going To*

Student: I**'m leaving** at midnight. That's my plan.

I**'m going to leave** at midnight. That's my plan.

Simple Present as Future

Soldier: I **leave** at midnight. Those are my orders.

Making Predictions

▶ 3 Use *be going to* to make predictions. Do not use the present continuous or the simple present as future to make predictions.

Future with *Be Going To*

They**'re going to win** tonight. Everyone thinks so.

x They're winning tonight. (INCORRECT)   x They win tonight. (INCORRECT)

It**'s going to rain** later.

x It rains later. (INCORRECT)   x It is raining later. (INCORRECT)

D1 Listening for Meaning and Use

▶ Notes 1A, 1B, 2A, 2B, 3

CD1 T17 Listen to each pair of sentences. Do they have approximately the same meaning or different meanings? Check (✓) the correct column.

	SAME	DIFFERENT
1.		✓
2.		
3.		
4.		
5.		
6.		

D2 Expressing Plans, Scheduled Events, and Predictions

▶ Notes 1A, 2A, 2B, 3

A. Build as many logical sentences as possible. Use an item from each column. Punctuate your sentences correctly. Which sentences are plans or scheduled events? Which sentences can only be predictions?

We're having a meeting tomorrow.

we're having we're going to have we have	a meeting a storm an exam an election a sale	tomorrow

B. Choose the nouns below that can appropriately begin the sentence. Which nouns would make the sentence illogical? Discuss each of your choices.

_____ begins tomorrow.

An explosion	My new job
It	School
A snowstorm	Winter vacation

D3 Discussing Plans and Scheduled Events

▶ Notes 1A, 1B, 2A, 2B

A. Work with a partner. Look at the European trip itinerary below and follow the instructions. When you are finished, switch roles for the Latin American trip itinerary.

Student A: You are the travel agent. Call your client and read the trip itinerary. Use the simple present as future to describe the itinerary.

Student B: You are the client. Take notes and ask questions.

Travel Agent: *You leave New York at 7:00 P.M. on July 5.*

Client: *What airline do I take?*

Travel Agent: *French Airways.*

European Trip Itinerary

July 5	Leave New York, Kennedy Airport (French Airways, Flight 139 at 7:00 P.M.)
July 6	Arrive Paris, Charles de Gaulle Airport 8:00 A.M. (Flight time: 7 hours)
July 6–11	Paris
July 11	Leave Paris, Charles de Gaulle Airport (Air Britain, Flight 267 at 11:00 A.M.) Arrive London Heathrow Airport 11:00 A.M. (Flight time: 1 hour, 15 minutes)
July 11–14	London
July 15–22	Car trip through Scotland
July 23	Return to London
July 24	Leave London Heathrow Airport (French Airways, Flight 278 at 12:00 P.M.)
July 25	Arrive New York, Kennedy Airport 3:00 P.M. (Flight time: 8 hours)

Latin American Trip Itinerary

August 19	Leave Los Angeles, LA International Airport (Skyway Airlines, Flight 299 at 7:20 A.M.) Arrive Mexico City International Airport 1:00 P.M.
August 19–21	Mexico City
August 22	Leave Mexico City International Airport (MexJet, Flight 137 at 7:04 A.M.) Arrive Buenos Aires, Ezeiza Airport, 8:16 A.M.
August 22–26	Buenos Aires
August 26	Leave Buenos Aires, Jorge Newbery Airport (Southern Air, Flight 201 at 11:15 A.M.) Arrive São Paolo, Guarulhos International Airport, 9:50 P.M.
August 26–31	São Paolo
September 1	Drive to Rio de Janeiro
September 1–7	Rio de Janeiro
September 8	Leave Rio de Janeiro, Galeão International Airport (Skyway Airlines, Flight 122 at 1:30 A.M.) Arrive Los Angeles, LA International Airport 2:10 P.M.

B. Send an email message to a friend who lives in one of the places you will be visiting in part A. Describe your itinerary and find out if your friend can meet you.

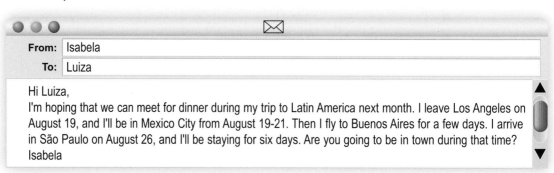

From:	Isabela
To:	Luiza

Hi Luiza,
I'm hoping that we can meet for dinner during my trip to Latin America next month. I leave Los Angeles on August 19, and I'll be in Mexico City from August 19-21. Then I fly to Buenos Aires for a few days. I arrive in São Paulo on August 26, and I'll be staying for six days. Are you going to be in town during that time?
Isabela

Contrasting *Will*, the Future Continuous, and *Be Going To*

Think Critically About Meaning and Use

A. Read the sentences and complete the tasks below.

1a. Don't be disappointed about the canceled ski trip. It'll snow soon.
1b. Wear your hat. It's probably going to snow.

2a. **Hanna:** Can someone open that window for me?
　　Shelley: I'll do it.
2b. **Kevin:** What's your decision about the job?
　　Laura: I'm going to do it.

1. **IDENTIFY** Underline the future verb forms in the sentences.

2. **ANALYZE** Which pair contrasts a quick decision with a plan thought about in advance?

3. **ANALYZE** Which pair expresses predictions that may or may not happen?

B. Discuss your answers with the class and read the Meaning and Use Notes to check them.

Meaning and Use Notes

ONLINE PRACTICE

Predictions and Expectations with Similar Meanings

▶ **1A**　*Will*, *be going to*, and the future continuous can be used to make predictions or state expectations with similar meaning. With predictions the speaker is less certain that an event will occur. With expectations, the speaker is more certain.

Predictions	Expectations
It **will warm up** tomorrow.	The bank **will close** early tomorrow.
It **will be warming up** tomorrow.	The bank **will be closing** early tomorrow.
It **is going to warm up** tomorrow.	The bank **is going to close** early tomorrow.

(Continued on page 66)

▶ 1B *Will* and the future continuous are frequently used in more formal contexts than *be going to*. Information in a more formal context is usually restated with *be going to* in conversation.

Future with *Will* and Future Continuous (More Formal)

      Sign: The bank **will close** at 1:00 P.M. today.

Weather Report: It **will be warming up** tomorrow.

Future with *Be Going To* (Less Formal)

Speaker: The bank **is going to close** at 1:00 P.M. today.

Speaker: It**'s going to warm up** tomorrow.

More Certain and Less Certain Predictions

▶ 2 With predictions, the meanings of *will* and *be going to* are sometimes similar, but not exactly the same. Use *be going to* when an event is fairly certain to happen very soon because there is evidence for it. Do not use *will* in this situation.

Future with Be *Going to* (More Certain Events)

They**'re going to win tonight**. They're the best team.

Look at the clouds. It**'s going to rain**.

Future with *Will* (Less Certain Events)

They**'ll win** tonight if they can keep the ball.

X Look at the clouds. It will rain. (INCORRECT)

Quick Decisions vs. Advance Plans

▶ 3 Especially in first person, *will* and *be going to* express different meanings. A sentence with *will* can express a quick decision or offer. However, the same sentence with *be going to* expresses a plan thought about in advance.

Future with *Will* (a Quick Decision)

A: Does anyone want to help me?

B: I**'ll help**. What can I do first?

Future with *Be Going To* (an Advance Plan)

A: What are your plans for the weekend?

B: I**'m going to help** my sister move tomorrow.

Ordering Events with Future Time Clauses

▶ 4 Future time clauses show the order of two future events. The specific order of events usually depends on the choice of the time word, not on the choice of future form. *Before, after, until, as soon as* (= right after), *by the time* (= before), and *when* introduce the time clause.

First Event	Second Event
I'm going to buy the novel	**before I get on the plane.**
After I buy the novel,	I'll get on the plane.
I'll be reading the novel	**until the plane lands.**
As soon as I get off the plane,	I'll get my bags.
I'll be in the baggage area	**by the time you get to the airport.**

> ! In sentences with *when*, the choice between using *will* or the future continuous can affect the order of events because the future continuous activity is in progress and the *will* activity is not.
>
> | First Event | Second Event | |
> |---|---|---|
> | **I'll be making** dinner | **when** you get home. | (I'll start dinner, and then you'll get home.) |
> | **When** you get home, | **I'll make** dinner. | (You'll get home, and then I'll start dinner.) |

E1 Listening for Meaning and Use

▶ Notes 1A, 1B, 2, 3

 CD1 T18 Listen to each situation. Choose the sentence that most appropriately follows what you hear.

1. (**a.**) That glass is going to fall.
   b. That glass will fall.

2. **a.** An agent is going to be with you shortly.
   b. An agent will be with you shortly.

3. **a.** I'm going to get it.
   b. I'll get it.

4. **a.** I'm going to read.
   b. I'll read.

5. **a.** I'll do it.
   b. I'm going to do it.

6. **a.** It will rain.
   b. It's going to rain.

7. **a.** Sure. I'll get it for you.
   b. Sure. I'll be getting it for you.

8. **a.** I'll work in an art museum.
   b. I'm going to work in an art museum.

E2 Restating Formal Announcements

▶ Notes 1A, 1B

Work with a partner. Decide in what context you might hear or see each sentence. Then use *be going to* to state each one in a less formal way.

1. The weather will be cool tomorrow with a chance of rain.

    Context: radio weather forecast

    Restatement: It's going to be cool tomorrow with a chance of rain.

2. Flight 276 will be arriving at Gate 12.

3. On April 1, the fare will increase to $1.75.

4. Classes will resume on January 22.

5. Tonight we will begin with a short poem.

E3 Restating Predictions

▶ Note 2

Work with a partner. Restate these predictions with *will*, if possible. Discuss why *will* would be inappropriate in some contexts.

1. I think that genetic engineering is going to become more widespread.

    I think that genetic engineering will become more widespread.

2. That car is speeding and the road is icy. The driver is going to lose control.

3. Computers are probably going to cost much less in a few years.

4. There are two seconds left in the hockey game. The buzzer is going to sound.

5. In a few years, "smart refrigerators" are going to tell owners when they need milk.

6. The patient's condition is improving. He's going to be fine.

E4 Making Quick Decisions and Stating Plans

▶ Note 3

A. Work in small groups. Brainstorm a list of what needs to be done for each situation. Then go around the group and have members volunteer for specific tasks using *will*.

1. Your kitchen is a mess. Your group has 15 minutes to clean it up before some important guests arrive.

    Benito: I'll clean the sink.
    Danilo: I'll sweep the floor.
    Mei: I'll…

2. Your group is going to have a potluck dinner tomorrow night.

3. Your group is going to have a garage sale to raise money for charity.

4. Your group will be going camping next weekend.

 B. Use your list for a chain summary of each situation in part A. First, restate your quick decision using *going to*. Then, restate the other volunteers' jobs with *be going to*.

> *Benito:* I'm going to clean the sink.
>
> *Danilo:* Benito is going to clean the sink, and I'm going to sweep the floor.
>
> *Mei:* Benito is going to clean the sink, Danilo is going to sweep the floor, and I'm going to...

E5 Understanding the Order of Future Events ▶ Note 4

A. Read these predictions. For each one, choose the situation that will happen or start first.

1. People will have more time after they open their home offices.

    a. People will have more time.

    (b.) They'll open their home offices.

2. We'll be doing all the housework until we get a robot.

    a. We'll be doing all the housework.

    b. We'll get a robot.

3. By the time our children are adults, most homeowners will be generating their own energy.

    a. Our children will become adults.

    b. Most howeowners will be generating their own energy.

4. We'll all own portable food testers as soon as they become easier to use.

    a. We'll all own portable food testers.

    b. They'll become easier to use.

5. We won't use electric cars until gas gets too expensive.

    a. We'll use electric cars.

    b. Gas will get too expensive.

6. We'll all buy videophones as soon as the prices go down.

    a. We'll all buy videophones.

    b. The prices will go down.

 B. Which predictions in part A do you think are likely to happen? Which ones are unlikely? Why? Discuss your opinions with your classmates.

E6 Verbs Expressing the Future

▶ Notes 1A, 1B, 2, 3

Work in small groups. Read each example and the sentences that follow. Choose the sentence that is closest in meaning to the example. Discuss your answers.

1. Yes, Jeanne, I'll pick up the children later. Don't worry.

   a. I'm about to pick up the children.

   b. I'm willing to pick up the children.

2. Watch out! That ladder is going to fall.

   a. The ladder will fall.

   b. The ladder is about to fall.

3. I'm going to visit my aunt this week. Would you like to come?

   a. I intend to visit my aunt this week.

   b. I promise to visit my aunt this week.

4. I'm meeting Susan at six.

   a. I'm willing to meet Susan at six.

   b. I plan to meet Susan at six.

5. I'll do it when I get home. You have my word.

   a. I promise to do it when I get home.

   b. I expect to do it when I get home.

6. **A:** No one volunteered to help me.

   B: I'll help.

   a. I'm willing to help.

   b. I'm about to help.

7. I won't clean up tonight. It's your turn.

   a. I don't expect to clean up tonight.

   b. I refuse to clean up tonight.

8. She's going to get the job. The boss was very impressed.

   a. I expect her to get the job.

   b. She intends to get the job.

9. He's starting graduate school in the fall.

   a. He plans to start graduate school.

   b. He's willing to start graduate school.

10. I'm going to China when I have enough money.

   a. I intend to go to China.

   b. I'm willing to go to China.

Beyond the Sentence

Repeating Future Forms in Discourse

In a paragraph or conversation, *be going to* or the future continuous often introduces the topic. The sentences that follow usually use the shorter forms *will* or the present continuous as future to supply more details.

I'm going to visit my aunt this afternoon. First, **I'll stop** at the bakery for her favorite cookies. Then **I'll pick up** my sister, and we**'ll get** on the interstate…

We**'re going to cook** a really nice dinner tonight. **I'm making** soup and a new pasta recipe. Kedra **is making** a salad, and Andrea **is baking** a cake.

Notice how several future forms can be used, but *will* is the most simple and the most common one to repeat as the paragraph progresses.

On Sunday, we**'re going to celebrate** my aunt's 40th birthday. We**'ll be taking** her out to her favorite restaurant where two of her friends **are joining** us. We**'ll order** her favorite meal and then, for dessert, we**'ll have** a cake with 40 candles. It**'ll be** fun to spend the afternoon with her.

E7 Repeating Future Forms in Discourse

Write a paragraph about something you are going to do in the next month, for example, take a trip or visit a friend. Be specific and explain exactly what you are going to do. Begin your paragraph with *be going to* or the future continuous, but use shorter future forms or other verbs to supply the details.

I'm going to visit my sister and her family in two weeks. I'll stop there on my way to a conference in San Francisco. We'll probably go out to dinner. We also intend to…

WRITING

Write a Blog Post About Life in the Future

Think Critically About Meaning and Use

A. Choose the best response to complete each conversation.

1. **A:** The milk spilled.
   B: I'll be getting a sponge. / (I'll get a sponge.)

2. **A:** Why can't you come to our house this weekend?
   B: I'll work. / I'll be working.

3. **A:** Why did you leave the door open?
   B: I'm going to carry in the packages. / I'll carry in the packages.

4. **A:** The doorbell is ringing.
   B: I'll answer it. / I'll be answering it.

5. **A:** I'm ready to take your order.
   B: I'll have a bowl of soup. / I have a bowl of soup.

6. **A:** Why did you turn on the oven?
   B: I'm making a cake later. / I'll make a cake later.

7. **A:** What are your plans for dinner?
   B: I'm going to cook pasta. / I'll cook pasta.

8. **A:** What does your work schedule say about next week?
   B: I'll work Monday and Thursday. / I work Monday and Thursday.

9. **A:** You'll have some free time in an hour.
   B: Maybe I'll do my homework. / Maybe I'll be doing my homework.

10. **A:** Who volunteered before to pick up the pizza for tonight's dinner?
    B: I did. I'll get it. / I did. I'm going to get it.

B. Discuss these questions in small groups.

1. **ANALYZE** Underline the verb forms in conversations 3 and 6. What do A's questions have in common? What do B's answers have in common?

2. **EVALUATE** Look at conversations 1, 3, and 6. In which one(s) does B use a future form to explain why something happened in the past? In which does B make a sudden decision to do something in the near future about something that happened in the recent past?

Edit

Find the errors in these paragraphs and correct them. There may be more than one way to correct an error.

One of the most exciting advances in medicine in the next few years is ~~gonna~~ *going* ~~be~~ *to be* the widespread use of robots in the operating room. Experts predict that "robot assistants" are never replacing surgeons. Nevertheless, there is no doubt that robots going to revolutionize surgery.

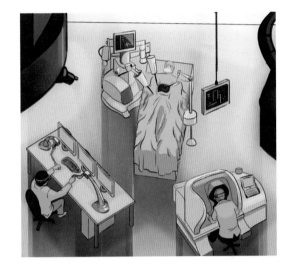

In just a few years, robots become the standard in certain types of heart surgery, eye surgery, hip surgery, and brain surgery. Why this is going to happen? The answer is simple. No surgeon will ever be able to keep his or her hand as steady as the hand of a robot. No surgeon is ever being able to greatly magnify a microscopic blood vessel with his or her own eyes. These are simple and routine tasks for medical robots.

Some patients are still worried, however. In the words of one patient before hip surgery, "How do I know the robot doesn't go crazy? Maybe it drills a hole in my head instead of my hip!"

Surgeons are quick to reassure their patients. "That's impossible," says one optimistic surgeon. "I promise that isn't happening. Robots are medical assistants. They'll work when I am going to give them a command, and they'll stop when I will say so. I be right there the whole time."

Write

Imagine you write for a trend forecaster's blog. The New Year is approaching and you've been thinking about the future, fifty years from now. Write a blog post about your predictions. *Use be going to, will, the future continuous, and future time clauses.*

1. **BRAINSTORM** Choose two areas (e.g., homes, education), and think about the changes that will occur. Use these categories to help you organize your ideas into paragraphs.

   • **Introduction:** What overall prediction can you make about life 50 years from now?
   • **Changes for the better:** What improvements will there be? What effect will these improvements have on the way we live? (Devote one paragraph to each area.)
   • **Challenges:** What old/new challenges will we be facing?
   • **Conclusion:** How optimistic are you about the future?

2. **WRITE A FIRST DRAFT** Before you write your first draft, read the checklist below and look at the predictions on pages 50–51 and 69. Write your draft using *be going to*, *will*, the future continuous, and future time clauses.

3. **EDIT** Read your work and check it against the checklist below. Circle grammar, spelling and punctuation errors.

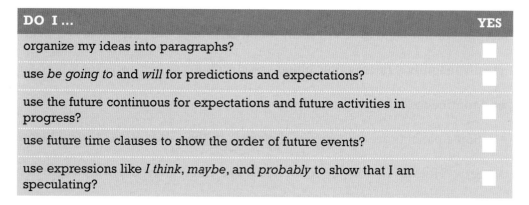

DO I ...	YES
organize my ideas into paragraphs?	☐
use *be going to* and *will* for predictions and expectations?	☐
use the future continuous for expectations and future activities in progress?	☐
use future time clauses to show the order of future events?	☐
use expressions like *I think*, *maybe*, and *probably* to show that I am speculating?	☐

4. **PEER REVIEW** Work with a partner to help you decide how to fix your errors and improve the content. Use the checklist above.

5. **REWRITE YOUR DRAFT** Using the comments from your partner, write a final draft.

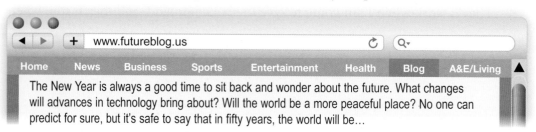

www.futureblog.us

Home | News | Business | Sports | Entertainment | Health | Blog | A&E/Living

The New Year is always a good time to sit back and wonder about the future. What changes will advances in technology bring about? Will the world be a more peaceful place? No one can predict for sure, but it's safe to say that in fifty years, the world will be...

Choose the correct word or words to complete each sentence.

1. What _____ at his corporate job?

   a. your father does
   b. do your father
   c. does your father do
   d. does your father

2. Passengers used to wait on long lines before the airlines _____ electronic check-in machines.

   a. introduce
   b. used to introduce
   c. introduced
   d. introducing

3. In what city _____ going to be?

   a. the next Olympic games will
   b. are the next Olympic games
   c. will the next Olympic games
   d. the next Olympic games are

What is expressed in each sentence? Choose the correct answer.

4. I'm living with John this semester.

   a. temporary situation
   b. habit
   c. general truth
   d. definition

5. My neighbors are always arguing. I can't sleep at night.

   a. schedule
   b. activity in progress
   c. definition
   d. complaint

6. When I ate the salad, I had an allergic reaction.

   a. interrupted event
   b. activity in progress
   c. cause and effect
   d. background info

7. My roommate was studying while I was reading.

   a. interrupted event
   b. simultaneous events
   c. habitual past
   d. sequential events

Choose the correct response to complete each conversation.

8. **A:** What time will you arrive tomorrow?
   B: _____

   a. I'm not sure. Probably late tonight.
   b. Yes, I'll be there by 10:00 A.M.
   c. The train arrives in Boston at 9:55 A.M.
   d. I will be arriving on Flight 472.

9. **A:** Where's Tanya?

   B: Look over there. _____

    a. Will you see her?   **c.** Yes, she certainly is.

    b. She walks towards us.   **d.** She's crossing the street.

10. **A:** Before I paid the bill, I complained to the manager.

   B: _____

    a. What did you complain about?   **c.** Why did you pay first?

    b. Who did you complain to?   **d.** What was he saying?

Change each statement into a question.

11. Her phone rang at 7:00.

   When _____

12. They watched the news last night.

   What _____

13. He lost 20 pounds on that diet.

   How many _____

Complete each sentence with the simple present form of the verb in parentheses. Use contractions when possible.

14. What _____ (usually/they/do) on Saturday night?

15. _____ (I/no/drink) coffee or tea because caffeine makes me jumpy.

16. _____ (you/feel) tired this morning?

17. Who _____ (know) Magda's new phone number? I need to call her.

Match the response to the statement or question below.

a. Sorry, I can't. I have to work.

b. No. If you need it, feel free to take it.

c. Will you return this book for me?
   I'd really appreciate it.

d. I know. I'll work harder next semester.

e. No, but I'll be reading it all weekend. I can't put it down!

f. I'll be studying for the college entrance exams.

_____ 18. Will you be using your car tomorrow?

_____ 19. If you're free, will you take me to the airport tomorrow?

_____ 20. What are your plans for the summer?

CHAPTER

4

The Present Perfect

The Questions That Stump the Scientists

A1 Before You Read

Discuss these questions.

Can you name some important scientific discoveries that happened recently? Why are they important? Do you think there are some questions that scientists will never be able to answer? What are they?

A2 Read

CD1 T19   Read this magazine article to find out what problems scientists still hope to solve.

The Questions That Stump The Scientists

We've come to "the end of science," writer John Horgan declared recently, saying that scientists have already made all the really
5 important discoveries. With future jobs on their minds, worried young scientists quickly responded with lists of what they don't know. After all, somewhere between the big
10 unanswerable problems, like the meaning of life and the very specialized subjects of most doctoral theses, there must be some questions that are both important and
15 answerable. An informal survey of a variety of young scientists produced some topics that might be worthwhile to look at:

Memory: How does the human brain
20 store knowledge? The brain is a physical organ, so does this mean that memory has a physical part too? We haven't discovered it yet, but if we do, the results will be earthshaking.
25 Consider some possibilities: Will we be able to find certain memories in the brain, change them, or move them from person to person? And now ask yourself this question: How many new
30 technologies and terrifying possibilities from science fiction can you imagine?

Missing Matter: Physicists have estimated the total amount of material in the universe, but they've observed only about 10 percent of it. Why can't they see the rest? For decades, they have believed that much of it is made up of an invisible substance known as dark matter. Experts say they are close to proving its existence and solving the mystery of its composition, but the moment of truth still hasn't arrived.

Are We Alone? It's a simple yes or no question. According to statistics, it's very likely that life has evolved elsewhere in the universe. However, we're still waiting for the first bit of convincing evidence of life somewhere else.

Have we reached the end of scientific discovery? "No way," says one young scientist from the University of British Columbia. Like most scientists, he cheerfully concludes that we've only just begun to make important discoveries. What do you think?

Adapted from *Newsweek*

---

doctoral theses: book-length papers written by university students to get advanced university degrees

matter: material that makes up the universe

physical: related to the body, not spiritual or mental

store: to collect and keep for later use

stump: to make someone unable to answer

A3 After You Read

Write *T* for true or *F* for false. Change the false statements to true ones.

___F___ **1.** John Horgan thinks we are just beginning to make important discoveries.

John Horgan thinks that we've come to the end of science.

_____ **2.** Young scientists think there are still many questions to study.

_____ **3.** Scientists know everything about the human brain.

_____ **4.** Scientists can move memories from one person to another person.

_____ **5.** Physicists are able to observe the whole universe.

_____ **6.** Scientists think there is probably life elsewhere in the universe.

B FORM

The Present Perfect

Think Critically About Form

A. Look back at the article on page 78 and complete the tasks below.

1. **IDENTIFY** Two examples of the present perfect are underlined. Find seven more examples.

2. **ANALYZE** What are the two different forms of *have* in these examples? When is each one used?

3. **CATEGORIZE** Sort your examples into regular and irregular verbs. How do you know the difference?

B. Discuss your answers with the class and read the Form charts to check them.

ONLINE PRACTICE

AFFIRMATIVE STATEMENTS		
SUBJECT + *HAVE*	**PAST PARTICIPLE**	
You**'ve**	**studied**	physics.
He**'s**	**done**	research.
They**'ve**	**found**	the answers.

NEGATIVE STATEMENTS			
SUBJECT	***HAVE* + NOT**	**PAST PARTICIPLE**	
You	**haven't**	**studied**	physics.
He	**hasn't**	**done**	research.
They	**haven't**	**found**	the answers.

YES/NO QUESTIONS			
HAVE	**SUBJECT**	**PAST PARTICIPLE**	
Have	you	**studied**	physics?
Has	he	**done**	research?
Have	they	**found**	the answers?

SHORT ANSWERS					
AFFIRMATIVE			**NEGATIVE**		
Yes,	I	**have.**	**No,**	I	**haven't.**
	he	**has.**		he	**hasn't.**
	they	**have.**		they	**haven't.**

INFORMATION QUESTIONS				
WH- WORD	*HAVE*	SUBJECT	PAST PARTICIPLE	
Where	**has**	he	**studied**?	
How long	**have**	they	**done**	research?

WH- WORD + *HAVE*			PAST PARTICIPLE	
Who's			**studied**	the problem?
What's			**happened**	lately?

- The past participle of regular verbs is the same as the simple past form (verb + *-ed*). See Appendices 4 and 5 for spelling and pronunciation rules for verbs ending in *-ed*.
- Irregular verbs have special past participle forms. See Appendix 6 for irregular verbs and their past participles.
- See Appendix 14 for contractions with *have*.

Do not confuse the contraction of *is* with the contraction of *has* in the present perfect.

He's **doing** research. = He **is doing** research. (He's currently doing research.)

He's **done** research. = He **has done** research. (He did research at some time in the past.)

Do not repeat *have/has* when present perfect verb phrases are connected by *and* or *or*.

He **has washed** his face and **brushed** his teeth.

B1 Listening for Form

 CD1 T20   Listen to the sentences and choose the one that you hear.

1. He's one of the racers. / He's won the race.

2. They called their senator. / They've called their senator.

3. Who's reading the book over there? / Who's read the book over there?

4. Where's the team playing this week? / Where's the team played this week?

5. She's worrying about her father. / She's worried about her father.

6. Who's going fishing? / Who's gone fishing?

7. You bought all of the equipment already. / You've bought all of the equipment already.

8. We looked up his telephone number. / We've looked up his telephone number.

B2 Identifying Past Participles

Choose the ten verb forms below each sentence that can correctly complete it.

1. I haven't _____ it.

   (caught)   cooked   eaten   found   had   saw   took

   chose   did   forgotten   gotten   heard   sung   written

2. It hasn't _____.

   appeared   broken   exploded   froze   happened   rained   sunk

   began   came   fallen   gone   left   started   tore

3. Why haven't you _____ it?

   allowed   cut   drank   driven   rang   spent   thrown

   bought   destroyed   drawn   kept   sang   taken   wore

B3 Building Present Perfect Sentences

Build as many meaningful sentences as possible. Use an item from each column. Punctuate your sentences correctly.

I have arrived early.

I she it have	have hasn't you	arrived early snowed a lot melted quickly been sick forgotten your umbrella bought herself anything

B4 Completing Conversations with the Present Perfect

 Complete these conversations with the words in parentheses and the present perfect. Use contractions when possible. Then practice the conversations with a partner.

Conversation 1

A: _Have you eaten_ (you/eat) in the new cafeteria yet?
            1

B: No, but I _____ (hear) that it's very good and very fast. It seems that
                        2

the dean finally _____ (begin) to understand that most students
                              3

don't have time for long lunch breaks.

Conversation 2

A: How long _____ (Tom/be) married?
                        1

B: He _____ (be) married for only a year, but he and his wife
                  2

_____ (know) each other since they were in college.
        3

Conversation 3

A: I _____ (not/send) my parents any email for a week. They probably
            1

think that something terrible _____ (happen) to me.
                                              2

B: I'm surprised that they _____ (not/call) or _____
                                          3   4

(write) you.

Conversation 4

A: We had a long list of things to do. What _____ (we/do) so far?
                                                            1

B: Well, we _____ (make) a lot of progress. So far, I
                        2

_____ (do) the laundry, you _____ (sweep) the
        3   4

kitchen, and Eric _____ (buy) the groceries. But we still
                              5

_____ (not/take) the clothes to the cleaners.
        6

Informally Speaking

Omitting *Have* and *You*

CD1 T21 Look at the cartoon and listen to the conversation. How is the underlined form in the cartoon different from what you hear?

> Have you seen any good movies lately?

> Yes, as a matter of fact. Last night I saw that new Japanese movie.

In very informal speech, *have* and *has* are often omitted from questions. The subject *you* may also be omitted if it is clear from the context.

Standard Form	What You Might Hear
Has she **been** here already?	"She been here already?"
Have you **talked** to your brother lately?	"(You) talked to your brother lately?"

B5 Understanding Informal Speech

CD1 T22 Listen and write the standard form of the words you hear.

1. _Have you heard_ any good jokes lately?

2. _____ your vacation yet?

3. _____ to the beach yet this summer?

4. _____ at that new restaurant yet?

5. _____ yet?

6. _____ my keys?

7. _____ any programming?

8. _____ you lately?

MEANING AND USE 1

Indefinite Past Time

Think Critically About Meaning and Use

A. Read the sentences and answer the questions below.

    a. I've traveled to Spain and Italy.   **b.** I traveled to Spain and Italy in July.

    1. ANALYZE Which sentence talks about a definite period of time in the past?

    2. DIFFERENTIATE In which sentence does the time seem less definite or less important?

B. Discuss your answers with the class and read the Meaning and Use Notes to check them.

Meaning and Use Notes

ONLINE PRACTICE

	Indefinite Past Time
▶ **1A**	The present perfect often expresses an action or state that happened at an indefinite time in the past. It does not express a definite time in the past; the action happened at any time up to the present.
	I**'ve read** that book. It's fascinating. **x** I've read that book a week ago. (INCORRECT)
	What **have** we **learned** about life? **x** What have we learned about life last year? (INCORRECT)
▶ **1B**	The action or state may occur only once or may be repeated several times.
	Ed **has been** to the exhibit <u>once</u>, but Al **has been** there <u>many times</u>.

	Adverbs Used with Indefinite Past Time
▶ **2A**	Adverbs such as *already*, *yet*, *still*, *so far*, *ever*, and *never* are frequently used with the present perfect to express the connection between the past and the present.
	We**'ve** <u>already</u> **eaten**. They <u>still</u> **haven't finished**.
	They **haven't found** the answers <u>yet</u>. <u>So far</u>, I**'ve visited** 16 countries.
▶ **2B**	Use *ever* to ask if an event took place at any time in the past. Only use negative forms of *ever (not ever, never)* in statements (not in questions).
	A: **Have** you <u>ever</u> **taken** a psychology course?
	B: I**'ve read** a few popular psychology books, but I**'ve** <u>never</u> actually **taken** a course.

C1 Listening for Meaning and Use

▶ Notes 1A, 1B, 2A, 2B

 CD1 T23 Listen and choose the best answer for each question.

1. a. Yes, I have.
    b. Twice.
    c. No, it hasn't.

2. a. Yes, several times.
    b. Here's one.
    c. No, she hasn't.

3. a. No, I haven't.
    b. She's coming soon.
    c. Yes, it has.

4. a. Not now.
    b. Yes, it has.
    c. Not yet.

5. a. No, never.
    b. No, she hasn't.
    c. No, I haven't.

6. a. No, not yet.
    b. Everything, except the laundry.
    c. I've already done it.

C2 Talking About Life Experiences with *Ever*

▶ Note 2B

 A. Work with a partner. Take turns asking and answering questions about your life experiences. Make questions with the expressions below and the present perfect with *ever*. Respond with a present perfect short answer and *Have you?*

1. have a flat tire

    A: *Have you ever had a flat tire?*
    B: *Yes, I have. Have you?* OR *No, I haven't. Have you?*

2. missed a flight

3. lose your wallet

4. run out of gas

5. tell a lie

6. meet a famous person

7. see a comet

8. ride a motorcycle

B. Follow these steps to ask your classmates about their life experiences.

1. Make up five questions with *Have you ever* to ask your classmates.

2. Move around the classroom and ask different classmates the questions. Return to your seat and tell the class what you have learned.

    I'm going to tell you about Paula. She has flown an airplane and...

C3 Making Up Reminders with Indefinite Past Time ▶ Notes 1A, 2A

A. List three or four things you need to do to prepare for each of these situations.

1. You are going to go to the supermarket.

check the refrigerator, make a shopping list,…

2. You have your first job interview tomorrow.

3. You have just picked out a used car to buy.

4. You are going to the park for a picnic.

 B. Work with a partner. Exchange lists and take turns. Use your partner's lists to make up reminders. Ask about what has been done for each situation. Use the present perfect and adverbs where appropriate.

Have you checked the refrigerator yet?
Have you packed the picnic lunch already?

 C. Take turns asking and answering the questions on your lists. Reply using short answers.

A: Have you checked the refrigerator yet?
B: Yes, I have. OR No, I haven't. I'll do it tomorrow.

C4 Writing About Accomplishments and Progress ▶ Notes 1A, 1B, 2A

 A. Choose an activity that you have already started planning (for example, a family reunion). Write sentences about your progress using the suggested adverbs and the present perfect. Then tell a partner about your progress.

1. Name three things that you've accomplished. Use *so far* or *already* in each sentence.

So far, I've made a list of the guests. OR
I've already made a list of the guests.

2. Name three things you still need to do. Use *still* or *yet*.

I still haven't invited the guests. OR
I haven't invited the guests yet.

B. Write a paragraph using your ideas from part A.

I am planning a family reunion for my grandmother's 80th birthday. So far, I have made a list of the guests, but I haven't invited them yet. I still haven't bought the invitations…

D MEANING AND USE 2

Recent Past Time and Continuing Time up to Now

Think Critically About Meaning and Use

A. Read the sentences and answer the questions below.

   a. I've worked for a publishing company.
   b. I've recently worked for a publishing company.
   c. I've worked for a publishing company for two years.

   1. EVALUATE Which sentence suggests that the speaker is still working for the publishing company?

   2. EVALUATE Which sentences suggest that the speaker doesn't work for the company anymore?

   3. EVALUATE Which sentence refers to the recent past?

B. Discuss your answers with the class and read the Meaning and Use Notes to check them.

Meaning and Use Notes

ONLINE
PRACTICE

Recent Past Time

▶ **1**   The present perfect often describes recent past actions and experiences, especially when their results are important in the present. Adverbs like *lately*, *recently*, and *just* emphasize this meaning of recent past time. (See the Vocabulary Notes on page 91 for more information about these adverbs.)

Conversations

A: Where**'s** your sister **been** <u>lately</u>?
    I **haven't seen** her.

B: She **hasn't been** home very much
    <u>recently</u>. She's busy looking for a job.

Announcements

Flight 602 from Miami **has landed** at Gate 4.

News Broadcasts

We**'ve** <u>just</u> **learned** that the mayor **has resigned**.

Telephone Recordings

The number you **have dialed**
    is busy.

Conclusions

(The doorbell is ringing.)
    I think the guests
    have (<u>just</u>) **arrived**.

Continuing Time up to Now

▶ **2A** The present perfect expresses actions and states that began in the past and continue at the present time. These sentences often have expressions with *for*, *since*, or *all* to indicate how long the situation has lasted.

A: **How long have** you **lived** here?

B: **I've lived** here <u>for twenty years</u>. (I still live here.)

I've lived here <u>since 1983</u>. (I still live here.)

I've lived here <u>all my life</u>. (I still live here.)

▶ **2B** Stative verbs like *be*, *have*, and *know*, and other verbs that can express duration, such as *keep* or *last*, are commonly used to express continuing time up to now.

We**'ve known** about it for a long time.

I**'ve kept** this secret for three months.

! Verbs that express an instant event such as *arrive*, *start*, *stop*, *hit*, or *realize* are not used to express continuing time up to now. However, they can be used with indefinite past time or recent past time.

Continuing Time up to Now   **Recent Past Time**

✗ We have arrived for an hour. (INCORRECT)   **We have** just **arrived**.

D1 Listening for Meaning and Use

▶ Notes 1, 2A

 CD1 T24   **A.** Listen to each sentence. Does the sentence express recent past time or continuing time up to now? Check (✓) the correct column.

	RECENT PAST TIME	CONTINUING TIME UP TO NOW
1.	✓	
2.		
3.		
4.		
5.		
6.		

(Continued on page 90)

CD1 T25 **B. Listen to each situation and the question that follows it. Choose the correct answer to the question.**

1. a. 10:00 A.M.
   b. 1:00 P.M.
   c. 11:00 A.M.
   d. 4:00 P.M.

2. a. All day.
   b. Since 5:00 P.M.
   c. This morning.
   d. For four hours.

3. a. 1:00 P.M.
   b. 3:30 P.M.
   c. 3:00 P.M.
   d. 2:00 P.M.

4. a. Since midnight.
   b. For three hours.
   c. For nine hours.
   d. For fifteen hours.

D2 Talking About Continuing Time up to Now ▶ Notes 2A, 2B

Work in groups of three. Switch roles for each phrase. When you are finished, think of two more phrases to ask about.

Student A: Ask a question using *how long* and a phrase below.

Students B and C: Answer using *for*, *all*, or *since*.

1. be in this room

   A: *How long have you been in this room?*
   B: *I've been in this room for ten minutes.*
   C: *I've been in this room all morning.*

2. know how to speak English

3. have your driver's license

4. own this book

5. be a student

6. live in your apartment / house / dorm

7. know the students in this class

8. own your car / bicycle

9. know how to use a computer

10. be in this city

Vocabulary Notes

Adverbs That Express Recent Past Time

Just means "right before now." It comes before the past participle.

> The mayor has **just** resigned.

Recently means "not long ago." It comes before the past participle, or at the beginning or end of the sentence.

> She's **recently** been away.   She's been away **recently**.
>
> **Recently**, she's been away.

Lately also means "not long ago." It comes at the beginning or end of the sentence.

> **Lately**, the weather has been awful.   The weather has been awful **lately**.

D3 Reaching Conclusions About Recent Past Time

 Work in small groups and look at the pictures. Make up sentences using *just*, *lately*, and *recently* to describe what you think has just happened.

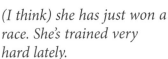
(I think) she has just won a race. She's trained very hard lately.

D4 Writing About Recent Past Events

▶ Note 1

A. These newspaper headlines tell about recent events. Use the information in the headline and the present perfect to complete the first line of each news article.

Mayor Powell Signs Antipollution Legislation

Research Center Receives Grant

Governor Miller Raises Gasoline Taxes

LOCAL GROCER SAVES CHILD'S LIFE

Geologist Makes Rare Discovery

1. For the second time in less than a year, Governor Miller _____*has raised*_____ _____*gasoline taxes*_____ by 5 percent.

2. Mayor Powell _____ that promises to reduce the amount of carbon monoxide in the air.

3. Douglas Lake, owner of Lake's Groceries, _____.

4. A geologist _____ in the William Robb State Forest, 20 miles west of the city.

5. The Human Behavior Research Center _____ to study the sleep patterns of children.

B. These sentences begin news articles. Write a related short headline with a simple present verb for each one.

1. Severe weather has caused serious delays at all major airports in the region.

   Severe Weather Causes Airport Delays

2. Technology stocks have risen sharply this week.

3. MCJ Industries has moved all of its offices to Texas.

4. State universities have lost millions of dollars in research grants this year.

5. President Perez has left for a 12-day trip to China and Japan.

Contrasting the Present Perfect and the Simple Past

Think Critically About Meaning and Use

A. Read the sentences and answer the questions below.

1a. I've worked in Los Angeles for three years. I love my job.
1b. I worked in Los Angeles for three years. I loved my job.
2a. When did you see the movie *Titanic*?
2b. Have you seen the movie *Titanic*?

1. **ANALYZE** Compare 1a and 1b. In which sentence does the speaker still work in Los Angeles? How do you know?

2. **ANALYZE** Compare 2a and 2b. Which sentence asks about the time of a past event? Which sentence does not ask about the time of a past event?

B. Discuss your answers with the class and read the Meaning and Use Notes to check them.

Meaning and Use Notes

ONLINE PRACTICE

Continuing Time up to Now vs. Completed Actions

▶ **1** The present perfect can express situations that continue at the present time, but the simple past can only express situations that are completed. The simple past can be used to talk about historical events, whereas the present perfect cannot.

Present Perfect	**Simple Past**
She's **been** slender all her life. (She is still alive and still slender.)	She **was** slender all her life. (She is no longer alive.)
I've **worked** there for ten years. (I still work there.)	I **worked** there for ten years. (I don't work there anymore.)
x Alexander Graham Bell has invented the telephone. (INCORRECT)	Alexander Graham Bell **invented** the telephone over 100 years ago.

(Continued on page 94)

Indefinite Past Time vs. Definite Past Time

▶ 2   Because present perfect sentences do not indicate a definite time, use the present perfect only to talk about an indefinite time. Use the simple past to talk about a definite time.

Present Perfect (Indefinite Past Time)	Simple Past (Definite Past Time)
Have you **visited** Maria lately?	**When did** you **visit** Maria?

Just, *Already*, and *Yet*

▶ 3   It is common to use *just*, *already*, and *yet* with the simple past. The following sentences have the same meaning.

Present Perfect	Simple Past
A: You should call Jada.	A: You should call Jada.
B: I've **just called** her.	B: I **just called** her.
A: Don't forget to buy some milk.	A: Don't forget to buy some milk.
B: I've **already bought** some.	B: I **already bought** some.
A: **Have** you **eaten yet**?	A: **Did** you **eat yet**?
B: No, not yet.	B: No, not yet.

E1 Listening for Meaning and Use   ▶ Note 1

CD1 T26   Listen to each situation and choose the sentence you hear. Pay attention to the second sentence in each situation to help you understand the context.

1. **a.** I've lived there for a year.
    b. (circled) I lived there for a year.

2. **a.** We've worked with him for six months.
    b. We worked with him for six months.

3. **a.** He's kept the secret all week.
    b. He kept the secret all week.

4. **a.** She's studied physics for two years.
    b. She studied physics for two years.

5. **a.** I've had a parrot for a long time.
    b. I had a parrot for a long time.

6. **a.** I've owned a car for years.
    b. I owned a car for years.

7. **a.** They've worked there for three years.
    b. They worked there for three years.

8. **a.** I've played the piano for years.
    b. I played the piano for years.

E2 Choosing the Simple Past or the Present Perfect ▶ Notes 1, 2

Choose the simple past or present perfect forms that best complete the conversation.

Jeff: How long ((have you had)/ did you have) this computer?

Kim: Let's see. (I've bought / I bought) it when (I've moved / I moved) here, so
(I've owned / I owned) it for a long time.

Jeff: Well, (I've had / I had) mine for two years, and it already seems to be outdated.
(It's been / It was) very slow lately. Do you think it needs more memory?

Kim: I don't know. (Have you called / Did you call) Janet lately? She knows everything
about this stuff. (She's worked / She worked) for Computing World since
(she's graduated / she graduated).

Jeff: Well, actually, I have tried to reach her. (I've phoned / I phoned) her last night, but
(she was / she's been) out for the evening.

Kim: What about your roommate? (Hasn't he taken / Didn't he take) all kinds of
engineering and computing courses last year?

Jeff: Yeah, but he doesn't know much about personal computing. Anyway,
(he's left / he left) town yesterday because his uncle (has died / died) suddenly
on Monday. (He lived / He's lived) with his uncle for two years. They were
very close.

Kim: Oh, I'm sorry to hear that. Why don't you call the Computer Center on campus?
(They were / They have been) very helpful last week when I called them.

Jeff: That's a good idea.

E3 Asking for Information

▶ Note 3

Work with a partner. Take turns as Student A and Student B. Imagine today is the town festival.

Student A: Ask about the festival events using the words in parentheses.
Student B: Answer the questions using the schedule.

GALESBURG TOWN FESTIVAL SCHEDULE

12:00–12:30	Welcome Speech by Mayor Ferrara
12:30–1:00	Jerry's Juggling Show
1:00–1:30	The Melodians Barbershop Quartet
1:30–2:00	Storytellers
2:00–2:30	Three-legged Race
2:30–3:00	Pie-eating Contest
3:00–3:30	Line Dancers from Green Apple Ranch
3:30–4:00	Folk-Dancing Club: Dances from Around the World
4:00–4:30	Jazz from the Blues Men
4:30–7:30	Picnic Dinner
7:30–8:00	Request-a-Song Sing-Along
8:00–8:45	Fireworks

1. It's 2:00 P.M. (the juggler/perform)

   A: Has the juggler already performed?   OR   *A: Did the juggler perform already?*
   B: Yes, he has. He finished an hour ago.   *B: Yes, he did. He finished an hour ago.*

2. It's 3:00 P.M. (the jazz band/play)

   A: Has the jazz band played yet?   OR   *A: Did the jazz band play yet?*
   B: No, they haven't. They play at four.   *B: No, they didn't. They play at four.*

3. It's 11:00 A.M. (the mayor/speak)

4. It's 5:00 P.M. (the picnic/start)

5. It's 7:00 P.M. (the fireworks/begin)

6. It's 3:00 P.M. (the three-legged race/happen)

7. It's 3:45 P.M. (the pie-eating contest/end)

8. It's 2:00 P.M. (The Melodians/sing)

9. It's 6:00 P.M. (the sing-along/take place)

10. It's 4:10 P.M. (the line dancers/perform)

Beyond the Sentence

Introducing Topics with the Present Perfect

The present perfect has a special introductory use in larger contexts. It is often used at the beginning of a written text (or conversation) to introduce a general idea with indefinite past time. The text often continues with the simple past to give more specific details about the general idea.

A Newspaper Article

For the second time in two weeks, an inmate **has escaped** from the local prison. Last night at 2:00 A.M., several guards **heard** strange noises coming from an underground tunnel. An investigation **revealed**...

E4 Introducing Topics with the Present Perfect

A. Read each present perfect introductory sentence. Then write a sentence in the simple past that adds a detail. Tell when the particular experience happened.

1. Computers have helped me a lot with my schoolwork. For example,

    I did all my assignments on a computer last semester.

2. There have been several disasters in recent years. For example,

    _____

3. I've made many mistakes in my life. For example,

    _____

4. There have been many changes in my country/town/family lately.

    For example, _____

5. I've learned a lot of important things in recent years. For example,

    _____

6. I've taken long trips by bus/train/car. For example,

    _____

B. Write a paragraph. Choose one of the six items in part A as the beginning of your paragraph. Use the simple past to develop specific examples and details.

Computers have helped me a lot with my schoolwork. For example, I did all my assignments on a computer last semester. I was able to type and edit my work quickly. Most importantly, I found a lot of useful information on the Internet without leaving home.

WRITING   Write a Newspaper Article

 Think Critically About Meaning and Use

A. Read each sentence and the statements that follow. Write *T* if the statement is true, *F* if it is false, or *?* if you do not have enough information to decide.

1. I've studied Russian.

   _F_   **a.** I'm still studying Russian.

   _T_   **b.** I studied Russian at some time in the past.

2. I haven't eaten breakfast this morning.

   _T_   **a.** It's still morning.

   _?_   **b.** I'm going to eat breakfast.

3. I've worked there for many years.

   _F_   **a.** I don't work there anymore.

   _?_   **b.** I'm changing jobs next week.

4. I still haven't visited the exhibit.

   _T_   **a.** I didn't visit the exhibit.

   _?_   **b.** I expect to visit the exhibit.

5. I've owned a house.

   _?_   **a.** I still own a house.

   _T_   **b.** I bought a house some time in the past.

6. I've had this cold for two weeks already.

   _F_   **a.** I don't have this cold anymore.

   _T_   **b.** I caught this cold two weeks ago.

7. I lived there for two years.

   _F_   **a.** I still live there.

   _F_   **b.** I moved two years ago.

8. I've already finished my work.

   _T_   **a.** I finished sooner than expected.

   _?_   **b.** I finished it a few minutes ago.

Edit

Find the errors in this newspaper article and correct them.

Hubble Celebrates 20 Years in Orbit

CAPE KENNEDY, April 22, 2010—Since 1993, the Hubble Space Telescope has ~~provide~~ *provided* us with extraordinary pictures of the universe. It has shown us new comets and black holes. It is found exploding stars. Astronomers have been amazed that the Hubble Space Telescope have sent back so many spectacular images. But it hasn't always been this way. The Hubble Space Telescope was actually been in space since 1990. However, for the first three years, there was a problem with the main mirror. The pictures that it sent back to earth were not at all clear. In 1993, two astronauts have fixed the problem. They took a space walk and dropped a special lens over the mirror. Since then, four other servicing missions helped to upgrade the telescope's scientific instruments and operational systems. The last of these has been in May of 2009.

Today the world celebrates Hubble's 20 years in orbit. Its images have delighted and amazing people around the world and its many discoveries have help to advance our understanding of the universe.

Write

Imagine you are a reporter. Write an article about a recent event or development in your community or country. Use the present perfect and other past, present, and future forms where appropriate.

1. **BRAINSTORM** Think about all the details you might want to include. Use these categories to help you organize your ideas into paragraphs:
   - **Introduce the event:** What has happened? What have one or more people said about the event or development?
   - **Describe the background:** What were things like before the event or development? What happened to bring it about?
   - **Analyze the significance:** Why is the event or development important? How is it affecting people at the current time? What impact will it have on the future?

2. **WRITE A FIRST DRAFT** Before you write your first draft, read the checklist below and look at the example on page 99. Write your draft using the present perfect.

3. **EDIT** Read your work and check it against the checklist below. Circle grammar, spelling, and punctuation errors.

DO I ...	YES
organize my ideas into two or three paragraphs?	☐
use the present perfect to introduce the topic?	☐
use the present perfect for indefinite past time, recent past time, and continuing time up to now?	☐
use the simple past to talk about completed actions and definite past time?	☐
use present and future forms, as needed, to discuss the short- and long-term effects?	☐

4. **PEER REVIEW** Work with a partner to help you decide how to fix your errors and improve the content. Use the checklist above.

5. **REWRITE YOUR DRAFT** Using the comments from your partner, write a final draft.

> TUTORING PROGRAM A GREAT SUCCESS
> For the past five years, secondary schools in our area have conducted a voluntary after-school teen-to-teen tutoring program, and up to now, according to School Superintendent Carmen Sanchez, the results have been amazing...

5

The Present Perfect Continuous

Longer Life in Blue Zones

A1 Before You Read

 Discuss these questions.

Do you look forward to old age? Why or why not? What are some things that people do in order to live longer and stay healthier?

A2 Read

CD1 T27 Read this book review to find out why people in some parts of the world are living longer and healthier lives than the rest of us.

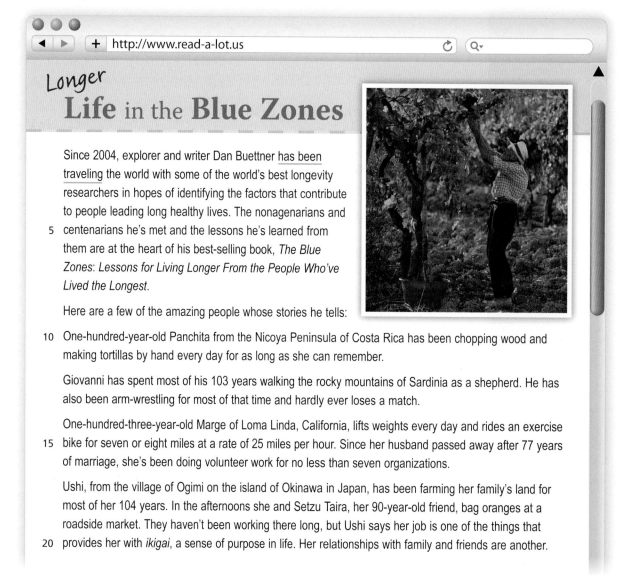

http://www.read-a-lot.us

Longer Life in the Blue Zones

Since 2004, explorer and writer Dan Buettner has been traveling the world with some of the world's best longevity researchers in hopes of identifying the factors that contribute to people leading long healthy lives. The nonagenarians and
5 centenarians he's met and the lessons he's learned from them are at the heart of his best-selling book, *The Blue Zones: Lessons for Living Longer From the People Who've Lived the Longest*.

Here are a few of the amazing people whose stories he tells:

10 One-hundred-year-old Panchita from the Nicoya Peninsula of Costa Rica has been chopping wood and making tortillas by hand every day for as long as she can remember.

Giovanni has spent most of his 103 years walking the rocky mountains of Sardinia as a shepherd. He has also been arm-wrestling for most of that time and hardly ever loses a match.

One-hundred-three-year-old Marge of Loma Linda, California, lifts weights every day and rides an exercise
15 bike for seven or eight miles at a rate of 25 miles per hour. Since her husband passed away after 77 years of marriage, she's been doing volunteer work for no less than seven organizations.

Ushi, from the village of Ogimi on the island of Okinawa in Japan, has been farming her family's land for most of her 104 years. In the afternoons she and Setzu Taira, her 90-year-old friend, bag oranges at a roadside market. They haven't been working there long, but Ushi says her job is one of the things that
20 provides her with *ikigai*, a sense of purpose in life. Her relationships with family and friends are another.

What do Panchita, Giovanni, Marge, and Ushi all have in common? The answer is simple. For their entire lives, they have been living in places that population scientists call Blue Zones—areas of the world where an unusually high percentage of the population live active, healthy lives past the age of 100.

Just how high is unusually high? Well, consider this. Experts estimate that in the United States there are
25　about 10–20 centenarians per 100,000 people. In Okinawa, the ratio is 50 per 100,000, probably the highest in the world. And in general, people in Blue Zones tend to live 10 years longer and experience a sixth the rate of heart disease, a fifth the rate of major cancers, and a third the rate of dementia than people who live elsewhere.

So what are the factors that contribute to greater longevity in the four Blue Zones? People who live in
30　all of these places share specific lifestyle habits that he calls the "Power 9." Among them: walking and getting regular exercise through activities of daily living, having a sense of purpose in life, eating wisely, making time to "de-stress" and relax on a daily basis, and enjoying strong, lifelong ties to one's family and community.

The Blue Zones is a must read for anyone who has ever asked: What can I do to maximize my chances of
35　leading a long, healthy life? Buettner's well-written book offers insight into how making small changes in our lifestyles might add years to our lives.

---

centenarians: people over 100 years old
dementia: medical condition characterized by loss
    of memory and a decline in mental ability
factors: elements that influence a particular result

longevity: long life
nonagenarians: people between 90 and
    99 years old
passed away: died

A3 After You Read

Complete these sentences with appropriate words.

1. The oldest person mentioned in the book review is from _____.

2. _____ recently got a part-time job at a roadside market.

3. Panchita gets her daily exercise by _____.

4. People who live in Blue Zones have lower rates of _____, cancer, and dementia than people from other places around the globe.

5. The Blue Zones covered in Buettner's book are the Nicoya Peninsula of Costa Rica, Sardinia, Loma Linda in California, and the island of _____ in Japan.

6. If you read the book, you will learn about Blue Zone lifestyle habits that Buettner refers to as the _____.

B FORM

The Present Perfect Continuous

Think Critically About Form

A. Look back at the book review on page 102 and complete the tasks below.

1. **IDENTIFY** An affirnative example of the present perfect continuous is underlined. Find five more affirmative examples and one negative example.

2. **RECOGNIZE** How many auxiliaries are there in each example? What ending is added to the main verb? Where is *not* placed in negative forms?

3. **ANALYZE** What are the two forms of *have* in your examples? When is each one used?

B. Discuss your answers with the class and read the Form charts to check them.

ONLINE PRACTICE

AFFIRMATIVE STATEMENTS

SUBJECT	*HAVE*	*BEEN*	VERB + *-ING*	
I	have			
She	has	been	working	there.
They	have			

NEGATIVE STATEMENTS

SUBJECT	*HAVE*	*NOT*	*BEEN*	VERB + *-ING*	
I	have				
She	has	not	been	working	there.
They	have				

YES/NO QUESTIONS

HAVE	SUBJECT	*BEEN*	VERB + *-ING*	
Have	you			
Has	she	been	working	there?
Have	they			

SHORT ANSWERS

YES	SUBJECT	*HAVE*	*NO*	SUBJECT	*HAVE + NOT*
	I	have.		I	haven't.
Yes,	she	has.	No,	she	hasn't.
	they	have.		they	haven't.

INFORMATION QUESTIONS					
WH- WORD	*HAVE*	SUBJECT	*BEEN*	VERB + *-ING*	
Who	**have**	you	**been**	**talking**	to?
How	**has**	she		**doing**?	

WH- WORD	*HAVE*		*BEEN*	VERB + *-ING*	
What	**has**		**been**	**happening**?	
Who				**calling**	you?

- The present perfect continuous has two auxiliary verbs: *have* and *been*. Only *have* and *has* form contractions.
- Verbs with stative meanings are not usually used with the present perfect continuous.

  x I have been knowing her. (INCORRECT)
- See Appendix 3 for spelling rules for verbs ending in *-ing*.
- See Appendix 14 for contractions with *have*.

B1 Listening for Form

CD1 T28 **Listen to the sentences and choose the one you hear.**

1. **a.** What's been happening this week?

   b. What's happening this week?

2. **a.** Jack has been visiting his grandparents.

   b. Jack has visited his grandparents.

3. **a.** It's rained all day.

   b. It's been raining all day.

4. **a.** They've been living in Florida.

   b. They're living in Florida.

5. **a.** He's been sleeping on the sofa.

   b. He's sleeping on the sofa.

6. **a.** She's been exercising at the gym.

   b. She's exercising at the gym.

B2 Completing Conversations with the Present Perfect Continuous

 Work with a partner. Complete these conversations with the words in parentheses and the present perfect continuous. Use contractions when possible. Then practice the conversations.

Conversation 1

A: What's wrong?

B: I _____'ve been trying_____ (try) to call the doctor for an hour, but the line is
           1

   still busy.

A: It's not an emergency, is it?

B: No, but I _____ (not/feel) well, and I'm starting to worry.
                   2

A: You do look tired. _____ (you/get) enough sleep?
                              3

B: Well, no, I really _____ (not/sleep) very well.
                              4

Conversation 2

A: I _____ (not/go) to the movies at all this summer.
             1

B: Why not?

A: I _____ (help) my parents almost every weekend.
             2

   We _____ (pack up) their house because they're
             3

   going to retire to Arizona next month. The house is very large, so it

   _____ (take) a lot of my time.
             4

Conversation 3

A: We normally don't get any homework in this course, but lately the

   instructor _____ (give) us an hour or two each night.
                   1

B: Maybe you _____ (not/make) enough progress, or maybe
                       2

   the material _____ (get) more difficult.
                     3

Conversation 4

A: You look wonderful. What _____ (you/do)?
                                       1

B: I _____ (exercise) a lot at the gym, and I
             2

   _____ (not/eat) junk food.
             3

B3 Unscrambling Questions

 A. Work with a partner. Reorder the words to form a question in the present perfect continuous. Make sure you use every word and correct punctuation.

1. you/how/been/have/lately/feeling

   How have you been feeling lately?

2. who/you/writing to/have/lately/been

3. recently/sleeping/you/well/have/been

4. been/you/working/semester/hard/this/have

5. enough/lately/you/exercising/been/have

6. time/what/recently/getting up/have/you/been

7. doing/you/what/in/the/been/have/evening

8. been/have/where/semester/you/eating/this/lunch

 B. Now take turns asking and answering the questions. Respond to each question and then ask *What about you?*

   A: How have you been feeling lately?
   B: I've been feeling fine. What about you?
   A: I've been feeling great.

B4 Writing Your Own Sentences

Use these verbs or your own to write two responses for each sentence below.

daydream	read	stand	talk	work
listen	sit	study	think	write

1. Describe something you have been doing since you came to class.

   I've been sitting in the back of the room. I've been…

2. Describe something you haven't been doing since you came to class.

3. Describe what two people in your class have been doing since they came to class.

4. Make questions about what your classmates have been doing since they came to class.

Omitting *Have*

CD1 T29   Look at the cartoon and listen to the conversation. How is each underlined form in the cartoon different from what you hear?

> Have you been going to the study sessions?

> No. I've been writing my English paper all week. It's due tomorrow.

In informal speech, some speakers may omit *have*. Other speakers may say *have* very quickly so that it is difficult to hear. This happens most often in statements with *I* and in questions with *you*. Notice that the subject *you* may also be omitted if it is clear from the context.

Standard Form	What You Might Hear
I **have been** studying so hard.	"I been studying so hard."
Have you **been doing** the homework lately?	"(You) been doing the homework lately?"

B5 Understanding Informal Speech

CD1 T30   Listen and write the standard form of the words you hear.

1. **A:** <u>What have you been doing</u> all day?

2. **B:** _____ my friend.

3. **A:** _____ OK?

4. **B:** No, _____ some problems with my back.

5. **A:** _____ at all?

6. **B:** _____ a lot.

Focus on Continuing or Recent Past Activities

Think Critically About Meaning and Use

A. Read the sentences and answer the questions below.

   a. Look at this library book. Someone has been writing all over it.

   b. She's been trying to find information on the Internet, and she's still searching for it.

   c. Look. It's finally done! I've been knitting this sweater for months.

   1. ANALYZE Which sentence focuses on an activity that began in the past and is continuing into the present?

   2. ANALYZE Which sentence is used to reach a conclusion about a current situation?

   3. ANALYZE Which sentence expresses an activity that was in progress but just ended?

B. Discuss your answers with the class and read the Meaning and Use Notes to check them.

Meaning and Use Notes

Focus on Continuing Activities up to Now
▶ **1** The present perfect continuous most often describes activities that began in the past and are continuing at the present time. The present perfect continuous emphasizes that the activity is ongoing. This meaning can be understood in context, but time expressions with *for* and *since* often help to show continuing time up to now.

I've been reading that novel, too. It's so good. (I'm still reading it.)

I've been writing this letter <u>since four o'clock</u>. (I'm still writing it.)

<u>For the past several years</u>, she**'s been knitting** a pair of mittens every day.
   (She's still knitting a pair every day.)

(Continued on page 110)

Focus on Continuing Activities up to Now

▶ 2 The present perfect continuous also describes recent situations or activities that were in progress, but have just ended. To emphasize the recent past, adverbs like *recently*, *just*, and *lately* may be used with the present perfect continuous.

I**'ve been thinking** about you <u>recently</u>.

I**'ve** <u>just</u> **been reading** the most wonderful book.

What **have** you **been doing** <u>lately</u>?

Common Uses of the Present Perfect Continuous

▶ 3 The present perfect continuous is frequently used to make an excuse along with an apology. It is also often used to reach a conclusion about a current situation.

An Excuse: I'm sorry I haven't called you. I **haven't been feeling** well lately.

A Conclusion: Half of my cake is gone. Someone **has been eating** it!

C1 Listening for Meaning and Use ▶ Notes 1–3

CD1 T31 Listen to the conversations between Max and Helen. Check (✓) the correct column to answer each question.

		MAX	HELEN
1.	Who is reading a John Grisham novel?	✓	
2.	Who is no longer sick?		
3.	Who still volunteers at a hospital?		
4.	Who has been to Chicago more than once this year?		
5.	Who has tried to call Eddie more recently?		
6.	Who is playing chess these days?		

C2 Making Apologies and Excuses ▶ Note 3

Work with a partner. Use the present perfect continuous to make excuses for your behavior. Begin with an apology. Then practice the conversations.

1. **A:** What's the matter? You're not listening to me.

    B: <u>I'm sorry. I've been thinking about something else.</u>

2. A: You're really late. What took you so long?

B: _____

3. A: I thought we were going to the movies sometime this week.

B: _____

4. A: You never come home right after school anymore. What's going on?

B: _____

5. A: Is something wrong? You keep looking out the window.

B: _____

6. A: It was your turn to go grocery shopping, wasn't it? We're out of milk.

B: _____

C3 Reaching Conclusions

▶ Note 3

 Work in small groups. Look at the picture. What can you conclude about what has just been happening? Write as many sentences as possible.

The TV is on. Someone has been watching TV.

C4 Writing Advertisements

▶ Notes 1, 3

A. Work with a partner. The advertisements below are missing introductory sentences that will attract attention. Write one or two present perfect continuous questions to begin each advertisement.

Have you been trying to lose

weight without success?

Have you been feeling

frustrated lately?

Come to
Diet Helpers

We'll help you lose weight easily
and healthily.

For more information call 555-2323.

1

_____

_____

_____

Call Apartment Finders Rental Agency at 555-4949.

We'll help you find the kind of apartment you need today.

3

_____

_____

_____

You need MORE EXERCISE!
Join the **Aurora Health & Fitness Club**

Reasonable rates,
friendly staff

Stop by for more information
about a free trial membership.

298 Ridgewood Road, 555-0908

2

_____

_____

_____

**You need to
get away!**

*We offer discounted plane
and bus fares for students.*

Let us help you plan your trip.

Mills Travel Agency
209 West Main St.

4

B. Create a newspaper, radio, or TV advertisement for one of the businesses below. Begin your advertisement with one or more attention-getting questions in the present perfect continuous. Be prepared to share your ad with the class.

a clothing store	an ice-cream shop	a photocopy center
a dance studio	an Internet provider	a take-out restaurant

D MEANING AND USE 2

Contrasting the Present Perfect Continuous and the Present Perfect

Think Critically About Meaning and Use

A. Read the sentences and answer the questions below.

1a. Kathy has been reading the book.   **2a.** I've been working here for ten years.
1b. Vera has read the book.   **2b.** I've worked here for ten years.

1. **EVALUATE** Which pair of sentences express the same meaning?

2. **EVALUATE** Which pair express different meanings?

3. **INTERPRET** In sentences 1a and 1b, who has probably finished the book? In which sentence is the activity continuing up to the present?

B. Discuss your answers with the class and read the Meaning and Use Notes to check them.

Meaning and Use Notes

ONLINE PRACTICE

Similar Meanings with Continuing Time up to Now

▶ **1A** Certain common verbs can be used in the present perfect or the present perfect continuous with *for* or *since* with no difference in meaning. These verbs include *live, teach, wear, work, study, stay,* and *feel.*

Present Perfect	Present Perfect Continuous
Mr. Ortiz **has lived** here since 1960.	Mr. Ortiz **has been living** here since 1960.
He**'s taught** English for a long time.	He**'s been teaching** English for a long time.
He**'s worn** the same jacket for years.	He**'s been wearing** the same jacket for years.

▶ **1B** The meanings of the present perfect and the present perfect continuous are not always the same. Sometimes the focus on the ongoing activity is stronger in the continuous, so you can choose the continuous to emphasize the length of time a situation lasted. Remember, using the continuous can show a more intense or emotional situation.

Present Perfect	Present Perfect Continuous
I**'ve waited** for an hour.	I**'ve been waiting** for an hour. I'm very annoyed.
I**'ve thought** about this for days.	I**'ve been thinking** about this for days. I can't stop.

(Continued on page 114)

Completed vs. Continuing or Recent Past Activities

▶ 2 The present perfect can express a completed activity that may or may not have been recent. In contrast, the present perfect continuous suggests that an activity is continuing up to the present time or was very recently completed.

Present Perfect	Present Perfect Continuous
I've read a book about astronomy. (I finished it at some indefinite time in the past.)	**I've been reading** a book about astronomy. (I'm not finished. OR I've just finished.)

A sentence with the present perfect continuous usually does not tell how many times an activity is repeated.

Present Perfect	Present Perfect Continuous
I've read the report three times.	**X** I've been reading the report three times. (INCORRECT)

D1 Listening for Meaning and Use

▶ Notes 1A, 1B, 2

 CD1 T32   **A.** Listen to each situation. Decide whether the situation is completed or continues. Check (✓) the correct column.

	COMPLETED	CONTINUES
1.		✓
2.		
3.		
4.		
5.		
6.		
7.		
8.		

D2 Contrasting the Present Perfect and the Present Perfect Continuous

▶ Notes 1A, 1B, 2

A. Complete this email with the words in parentheses and the present perfect or the present perfect continuous. In some sentences, either one is acceptable.

From: Anne Atherton
To: Ellen Bates
Subject: Hello!

Dear Ellen,

How are you and how's your family? _Has your father been feeling_
                                                                    1
(your father/feel) better? I hope so. I _____ (think) about you a lot and
                                                       2
_____ (wonder) if everything is OK.
       3

I _____ (read) the novel that you sent me for my birthday. So far, I
         4
_____ (read) about a hundred pages, and I'm really enjoying it. I
       5
_____ (be) so busy lately that I _____ (not/have) much
       6   7
time to read, but I hope to finish it soon.

Right now, I'm writing a paper for my psychology course. I _____
                                                                              8
(write) it for two weeks. It's going to be long. So far, I _____ (change)
                                                                  9
the topic four times, but now I'm finally pleased with it.

What _____ (you/do) during the past few weeks? _____
              10   11
(you/work) hard? _____ (you/have) any exams yet? I
                          12
_____ (have) two so far, and I did pretty well on them.
       13

_____ (you/decide) what you're going to do this summer? We really
       14
need to make plans soon! Please write!

Love,
Anne

B. Reread the email in part A. Write a similar email to a family member or friend. Use the present perfect and the present perfect continuous to tell what you have been doing recently and to ask questions, too.

D3 Writing a Conversation

 Work in small groups. Have you ever exaggerated in order to impress someone or to avoid a problem? Choose one of these situations and write a conversation in which one of the characters exaggerates. Use the present perfect and the present perfect continuous. Act out your conversation to the class.

1. A young man is trying to impress some new friends that he has just met. Although he has just begun a low-paying job at a television station, he exaggerates quite a bit about his job.

   New Friend: *So what do you do?*
   Young Man: *I work for XYZ News. I haven't been there long, but I've been working very hard. I've been writing all of the stories for the news show. I've also been on television three times.*

2. A young woman is at a job interview for a well-paying job. She is not qualified for this job. She has not finished college. She has only worked in her uncle's law office for a few months where she answers the telephone and runs errands.

3. A man is on the phone with his mother, who will soon be celebrating her 50th birthday. He and his brothers and sisters are planning a surprise birthday celebration. The mother is getting suspicious and asking a lot of questions.

4. A teenager promises that she will make dinner while her parents pick up relatives at the airport. They call from the airport to check on her progress. She assures them that she has been very busy. In fact, she hasn't really started dinner yet.

Beyond the Sentence

Connecting the Past and the Present in Discourse

In longer conversations and in writing, it is often important to relate past and present situations and events. Choose between the simple past, the present perfect, and the present perfect continuous to focus on whether a situation is complete or incomplete, recent or distant, whether it happened once or many times, and how long it lasted.

   A: I**'ve been working** here for nine years, and that's how long I**'ve known** Jenny. This is where we **met**.

   B: How long **did** you **know** each other before you **got** married?

   A: For a year.

   B: So you**'ve been married** for eight years. It doesn't seem that long.

   A: Well, we just **celebrated** our eighth wedding anniversary. We **spent** the weekend in the mountains…

D4 Connecting the Past and the Present in Discourse

Complete this conversation by choosing the correct answers in parentheses. In some sentences, either answer is possible.

Daughter: (I've been studying / I studied) French (for / since) six years now, but
₁ ₂
lately (I thought / I've been thinking) that I don't want to be a French
₃
teacher. You see…

Mother: But what about your plans to study in Paris next year? I thought
(you made / you've made) your decision a few months ago to apply for
₄
the Junior Year Abroad program.

Daughter: Yes, (I've applied / I've been applying) for that, and I'd still like to go!
₅
You see…

Mother: But what's the point of going to Paris if you've already
(decided / been deciding) not to be a French teacher?
₆

Daughter: (I tried / I've been trying) to tell you… You see,
₇
(I took / I've been taking) a course in French Art this term, and I'm
₈
really enjoying it. In fact, I want to change my major to Art History and
then minor in French.

Mother: And have you (told / been telling) your advisor this?
₉

Daughter: Of course! (I talked / I've talked) to her a month ago when I first
₁₀
started to think about it, and (I spoke / I've spoken) to her every week
₁₁
since then. (She's been / She was) very helpful in showing me how I can
₁₂
combine my two interests.

Mother: So, is it official? Have you (changed / been changing) your major yet?
₁₃

Daughter: No, (I decided / I've been deciding) to talk to you first. That's why
₁₄
(I've come / I've been coming home) this weekend! So what do
₁₅
you think?

Mother: Well, (I've never seen / I never saw) you so excited, so I think it's a
₁₆
great idea!

WRITING   Write a Letter to the Editor

Think Critically About Meaning and Use

A. Choose the best response to complete each conversation.

1. A: I've been working at this school for 15 years.
    B: a. Why did you leave?
        b. Are you going to retire soon?

2. A: Andrew has been visiting us for three days.
    B: a. Is he having a good time?
        b. Did he have a good time?

3. A: Cheryl has been going to Vancouver on business.
    B: a. How many times has she been there?
        b. Has she gone there more than once?

4. A: Excuse me, Miss. I've been waiting for the doctor for an hour.
    B: a. How long have you been here?
        b. He had an emergency. He'll be with you soon.

5. A: Joanna has been coming to work late.
    B: a. It's happened only once. Can't we ignore it?
        b. It's happened more than once. We can't ignore it.

6. A: How long have you known about the scandal?
    B: a. A few minutes ago.
        b. Since I saw it in the newspaper.

B. Discuss these questions in small groups.

1. EVALUATE Find the conversations that start with the present perfect continuous. In which one of these could speaker A have used the present continuous without changing the meaning of the statement or question?

2. DRAW A CONCLUSION Look at conversation 3. How does the meaning change if speaker A had said, "Cheryl has gone to Vancouver on business?"

Edit

Find the errors in this paragraph and correct them. Pay close attention to the context of each sentence.

Life expectancy is the average number of years that a person will live. Two thousand years ago, the Romans have been living ~~lived~~ only an average of 22 years. In other words, they have been having a life expectancy of 22. Since the beginning of the twentieth century, life expectancy around the world has been rising dramatically in many parts of the world. It will certainly continue to go up well into the twenty-first century. The rise in life expectancy has been being due to the fact that people have been taking much better care of themselves. Each generation has experienced better nutrition and medical care than the one before. In 1900 people in the United States have been living to an average age of 47. All that has changed, however: The life expectancy in 2009 was 78.7, and it may be even higher today.

Write

More and more people have been living to the age of 80 and beyond. Do you think your country has been doing a good job of taking care of its elderly population? Write a letter to the editor of your local newspaper expressing your opinion. Use the present perfect continuous and other past, present, and future forms where appropriate.

1. **BRAINSTORM** Use these questions to help you organize your letter into paragraphs.
   - What has the government been doing to help elderly people in recent years? (Think about services such as housing, finances, health, and recreation.)
   - What problems have elderly people and their younger relatives been experiencing with these services? How will the situation worsen in the future?
   - What do you think the role of the government should be in the future?

2. **WRITE A FIRST DRAFT** Before you write your first draft, read the checklist below and look at the examples on page 119. Write your draft using the present perfect continuous.

3. **EDIT** Read your work and check it against the checklist below. Circle grammar, spelling, and punctuation errors.

DO I ...	YES
organize my ideas into paragraphs?	☐
use affirmative and negative statements in the present perfect continuous?	☐
use the present perfect continuous for continuing time up to now and recent past activities?	☐
use other tenses as necessary to talk about the present and future?	☐

4. **PEER REVIEW** Work with a partner to help you decide how to fix your errors and improve the content. Use the checklist above.

5. **REWRITE YOUR DRAFT** Using the comments from your partner, write a final draft.

> Dear Editor,
>
> I am writing to express my concerns about the services that the government provides for the elderly. While it is true that our culture has a long tradition of caring for the elderly, people have been living longer and...

6

The Past Perfect and the Past Perfect Continuous

Wild Thing

A1 Before You Read

Discuss these questions.

Have you ever wanted to do something different or unusual, such as climbing a mountain or bungee jumping? Name some challenges that you would like to face. Why do some people like to face great challenges?

A2 Read

CD1 T33 **Read this book excerpt to find out why a young woman wanted to participate in an educational program called Outward Bound.**

Wild Thing

With the wind biting my face and rain soaking through my clothes, it didn't seem like July. I watched a puddle form at the foot of my 5 sleeping bag as the 10-foot plastic sheet above me gave way to the wind. I hadn't eaten for almost a day, and a rumble in my stomach demanded to know why I was in the 10 Northern Cascades of Oregon—alone, soaked—in the first place. With two more days alone in the wilds ahead of me, I had plenty of time to think about that question.

15 I'd always admired people who had been in Outward Bound, basically because I'd always lumped myself in the I-could-never-do-that category. For one thing, I just assumed I was 20 too small and urban… I also wasn't a big risk-taker. I'd always relied a lot

on my family and friends, and I evaluated myself on how well I met their expectations of me.

25   Signing up for an Outward Bound course the summer after my junior year in high school was a chance to break away from that. After all, the courses are described as "adventure-
30 based education programs that promote self-discovery through tough outdoor activities." Exactly what I needed; I would be facing challenges away from my usual supporters. As
35 the starting date approached, though, I became increasingly terrified. I'd never attempted mountain climbing, white-water rafting, backpacking, rappelling, or rock climbing, and I
40 was plagued by fears that I would fail at one or all of them. I begged my mother to cancel for me. No such luck…

Adapted from *Chicken Soup for the Teenage Soul*

lump: to put many things into one category
plagued: continuously upset or troubled
rappelling: using ropes to climb down a steep mountain

rely on: to depend on
rumble: a deep, rolling sound
wilds: wilderness; a natural area with few people

A3 After You Read

Write *T* for true or *F* for false for each statement.

___T___ **1.** The young woman was going to spend two more days alone in the wilderness.

_____ **2.** She came from the city.

_____ **3.** She had always been very self-confident.

_____ **4.** It was summer.

_____ **5.** She was an expert mountain climber.

_____ **6.** Her mother wanted her to stay home.

B FORM

The Past Perfect and the Past Perfect Continuous

Think Critically About Form

A. Look back at the book excerpt on page 122 and complete the tasks below.

1. **IDENTIFY** An example of the past perfect is underlined. Find four more examples. What is the contracted form of *had* in the past perfect?

2. **COMPARE AND CONTRAST** Look at the following example of the past perfect continuous. Underline the two auxiliaries and circle the main verb. How does it differ from the past perfect?

    She had been searching for a way to challenge herself.

B. Discuss your answers with the class and read the Form charts to check them.

▶ The Past Perfect

ONLINE PRACTICE

AFFIRMATIVE STATEMENTS			
SUBJECT	**HAD**	**PAST PARTICIPLE**	
I			
He	**had**	**hiked**	for hours by then.
They			

CONTRACTION		
He**'d**	**hiked**	for hours by then.

NEGATIVE STATEMENTS				
SUBJECT	**HAD**	**NOT**	**PAST PARTICIPLE**	
I				
He	**had**	**not**	**hiked**	before.
They				

CONTRACTION		
He	**hadn't**	**hiked**	before.

▶ The Past Perfect Continuous

AFFIRMATIVE STATEMENTS				
SUBJECT	**HAD**	**BEEN**	**VERB + -ING**	
I				
He	**had**	**been**	**hiking**	for hours by then.
They				

CONTRACTION			
He**'d**		**been**	**hiking**	for hours by then.

NEGATIVE STATEMENTS					
SUBJECT	**HAD**	**NOT**	**BEEN**	**VERB + -ING**	
I					
He	**had**	**not**	**been**	**hiking**	before.
They					

CONTRACTION				
He	**hadn't**		**been**	**hiking**	before.

▶ The Past Perfect

YES/NO QUESTIONS			
HAD	**SUBJECT**	**VERB**	
Had	you / he / they	**hiked**	before?

SHORT ANSWERS						
YES	**SUBJECT**	*HAD*	*NO*	**SUBJECT**	*HAD + NOT*	
Yes,	I / he / they	**had.**	**No,**	I / he / they	**hadn't.**	

INFORMATION QUESTIONS				
WH-WORD	*HAD*	**SUBJECT**	**PAST PARTICIPLE**	
Where	had	you	**hiked**	before?
What	had	he	**done?**	

WH-WORD	*HAD*	PAST PARTICIPLE
What	**had**	**happened?**

▶ The Past Perfect Continuous

YES/NO QUESTIONS				
HAD	**SUBJECT**	*BEEN*	**VERB + -ING**	
Had	you / he / they	**been**	**hiking**	before?

SHORT ANSWERS						
YES	**SUBJECT**	*HAD*	*NO*	**SUBJECT**	*HAD + NOT*	
Yes,	I / he / they	**had.**	**No,**	I / he / they	**hadn't.**	

INFORMATION QUESTIONS					
WH-WORD	*HAD*	**SUBJECT**	*BEEN*	**VERB + -ING**	
Why	had	you	been	**hiking**	before?
Where	had	he	been	**doing?**	

WH-WORD	*HAD*		VERB + -ING
What	**had**	**been**	**happening?**

The Past Perfect

- The past perfect has the same form with all subjects.
- The past participle of regular verbs is the same as the simple past form (verb + -*ed*). See Appendices 4 and 5 for spelling and pronunciation rules for verbs ending in -*ed*.
- Irregular verbs have special past participle forms. See Appendix 6 for irregular verbs and their past participles.
- See Appendix 14 for contractions with *had*.
- Note that the past perfect form of *have* is *had had*. It is an irregular form.

  It was 2:00 P.M. We **had had** a busy day at the store, and I was exhausted.

(Continued on page 126)

The Past Perfect Continuous

- The past perfect continuous has two auxiliary verbs: *had* and *been*. Only *had* forms contractions.
- Verbs with stative meanings are not usually used with the past perfect continuous.

  I **had** already **known** him for many years.

  x I had already been knowing him for many years. (INCORRECT)

- See Appendix 3 for spelling rules for verbs ending in *-ing*.

B1 Listening for Form

CD1 T34   **Listen and write the simple past, past perfect, or past perfect continuous verb forms you hear. Use full forms or contractions.**

In 1928, Amelia Earhart _____became_____
                                    1
the first woman to fly across the Atlantic. Ten years

before, she _____ as a nurse's aide
                      2

when she _____ an airfield near
                   3

Toronto. She _____ her mind that
                      4

she _____ to fly an airplane right
               5

then. After her trans-Atlantic flight, Ms. Earhart

_____ an instant heroine, although she really _____
           6   7

the plane. Her two male companions _____ her touch any of the
                                               8

controls. But the world _____.
                                 9

Charles Lindbergh _____ the Atlantic a year earlier, and many
                              10

aviators _____ to repeat his successful flight since then. Sadly, fourteen
                11

pilots, including three women, _____ since Lindbergh's triumph.
                                          12

Because Ms. Earhart _____ embarrassed about her role in her first
                                13

trans-Atlantic flight, she _____ more determined than ever to fly across
                                   14

the Atlantic alone. And that's exactly what _____ in 1932 when she
                                                         15

finally _____ over the Atlantic by herself.
               16

B2 Working on Verb Forms

Complete the chart.

	SIMPLE PAST	PAST PERFECT	PAST PERFECT CONTINUOUS
1.	I flew home.	I had flown home.	I had been flying home.
2.		We had gone to school.	
3.			They had been trying hard.
4.	I held my keys.		
5.			You had been having fun.
6.	He made a mess.		
7.		They had thought about it.	
8.			We had been doing nothing.
9.	What happened?		
10.		It had gotten harder.	

B3 Building Sentences

Build as many meaningful sentences as possible. Use an item from each column. Punctuate your sentences correctly.

Had you been working?

had you	been	working
she	had	left
who	had been	lunch
		sick
		taken a walk

B4 Asking and Answering Questions

 A. Work with a partner. Take turns asking and answering questions using the phrases below and the past perfect. Start your questions with *Before you started this course* and use *ever*. Respond with short answers and an explanation.

1. take any other English courses

   A: *Before you started this course, had you ever taken any other English courses?*

   B: *Yes, I had. I'd studied English for a year in high school.* OR
   No, I hadn't. I'd never taken any English courses.

2. study English grammar

3. speak on the phone in English

4. write any letters in English

5. see any English-language movies

 B. Now take turns asking and answering questions using the phrases below and the past perfect continuous. Start your questions with *Before you started this course*. Respond with short answers and an explanation.

1. read any English-language newspapers

   A: *Before you started this course, had you been reading any English-language newspapers?*

   B: *Yes, I had. I'd been reading The New York Times almost every day.* OR
   No, I hadn't.

2. learn any songs in English

3. practice English with friends

4. watch any TV programs in English

5. listen to English-language news broadcasts

B5 Transforming Sentences

Change the past perfect continuous to the past perfect. Where possible, change the past perfect to the past perfect continuous. Which sentences cannot change? Why?

1. We had been standing outside for a long time.

   We had stood outside for a long time.

2. I had never had a car with so many problems.

3. She had been limping for the last mile.

4. How long had they known about the accident?

5. Where had everybody been?

6. Had anyone been looking for us?

7. They had been trying to call for help.

8. What had happened?

💬 Informally Speaking

Reduced Forms of *Had*

 CD1 T35 Look at the cartoon and listen to the conversation. How is the underlined form in the cartoon different from what you hear?

Especially in fast speech, *had* is usually reduced with subject nouns. *Had* is also reduced with many information question words.

Did you see Dana and Maria at the library last night?

Dana had already left by the time I got there, but I saw Maria.

Standard Form	What You Might Hear
Dana had already left.	"/ˈdænəd/ already left."
The **cars had** stopped.	"The /ˈkɑrzəd/ stopped."
Who had already left?	"/hud/ already left?"
What had you been doing?	"/ˈwʌtəd/ you been doing?"

B6 Understanding Informal Speech

🔊 CD1 T36 **Listen and write the standard form of the words you hear.**

1. She __had__ never __been__ alone in the woods before.

2. Her family _____ camping when she was young.

3. Her father _____ her the skills she needed.

4. No one _____ her for this experience, though.

5. Why _____ she _____ for this program?

6. Who _____she _____ to impress?

C MEANING AND USE 1

The Past Perfect

Think Critically About Meaning and Use

A. Read the sentences and complete the tasks below.

    a. I called for help because a tree had fallen across my driveway.
    b. She wanted to withdraw from the course after she had enrolled.
    c. He'd been on a mountain climbing expedition before he wrote the article.
    d. Although I'd been terrified, I felt quite brave the next morning.

Think about the two events in each sentence.

    1. IDENTIFY Underline the clause that expresses the earlier event.

    2. RECOGNIZE What verb form is in the clause that expresses the earlier event?

    3. RECOGNIZE What verb form is in the clause that expresses the later event?

B. Discuss your answers with the class and read the Meaning and Use Notes to check them.

Meaning and Use Notes

ONLINE PRACTICE

Order of Events in the Past

▶ **1A** The past perfect expresses the relationship in time between two past events. It shows that one action or state occurred before another action or state in the past. The past perfect expresses the first (or earlier) event. The simple past often expresses the second (or later) event.

Past Perfect (1st Event)	Simple Past (2nd Event)
I **had** just **completed** the exam.	I **felt** so relieved.

▶ **1B** The past time can be recent or distant.

Recent Time

Miguel called me <u>this morning</u>, but I wasn't there. I**'d gone** to a meeting.

Distant Time

Miguel wrote me <u>last year</u>, but I never got the letter. I**'d moved** away.

The Past Perfect and Past Time Clauses

▶ **2A** The past perfect is often used in sentences containing past time clauses. The past perfect is used to indicate the first event. The simple past is used to indicate the second event. *Before*, *by the time*, *when*, *until*, and *after* introduce the time clause.

Past Perfect (1st Event)	Simple Past (2nd Event)
The thief **had escaped**	<u>before</u> I **called** the police.
We **had calmed** down	<u>by the time</u> the police **came**.
He **had been** upstairs	<u>when</u> we **came** home.
We **hadn't noticed**	<u>until</u> we **heard** the footsteps.
<u>After</u> I **had called** the police,	we **realized** the thief was gone.

▶ **2B** In sentences with *before*, *after*, *by the time*, and *until*, the past perfect is sometimes replaced by the simple past with no difference in meaning. This is especially common with *before* and *after*.

Past Perfect and Simple Past		Simple Past Only
I**'d gone** inside before I **took off** my coat.	=	I **went** inside before I **took off** my coat.
After I**'d gone** inside, I **took off** my coat.	=	After I **went** inside, I **took off** my coat.

Expressions Used with the Past Perfect

▶ **3A** The past perfect is often used with the same adverbs and prepositions that are used with the present perfect: *already*, *yet*, *still*, *ever*, *never*, *for*, *since*, and *just*. These expressions help to clarify the sequence of past events.

By lunchtime, we **had** <u>already</u> **discussed** the new budget and written a report. We **hadn't written** the new vacation policy <u>yet</u>.

I **had lived** in Texas <u>for 12 years</u> before I moved to California.

A: **Had** she <u>ever</u> **traveled** abroad before she went to college?

B: No, she**'d** <u>never</u> **left** her hometown.

▶ **3B** *By* + a time can be used with the past perfect to express the later time in the sentence.

We **had finished** <u>by then</u>.

<u>By noon</u>, we **had hiked** two miles.

C1 Listening for Meaning and Use

▶ Notes 1A, 1B, 2A, 2B, 3B

CD1 T37 Listen to the sentences. For each pair of past events below, choose the event that happened first.

1. (a.) The patient's condition improved.
   b. The doctor came.

2. a. We got to the airport.
   b. The plane landed.

3. a. I entered the building.
   b. I took off my hat.

4. a. The emergency crew arrived.
   b. The building collapsed.

5. a. I saw Betty.
   b. She heard the news.

6. a. He became vice president.
   b. He worked hard.

7. a. I called my mother.
   b. I spoke to my sister.

8. a. She hurt her wrist.
   b. She went to work.

C2 Expressing the Order of Past Events

▶ Notes 1A, 1B, 2A, 2B

Read the pairs of sentences and order the events. Number the first event with a *1* and the second with a *2*. Then make a sentence with the word(s) in parentheses that includes both events. Use the past perfect and the simple past where appropriate.

1. __2__ The sink overflowed.   __1__ I left the water running.

   (after) _The sink overflowed after I had left the water running._

2. _____ He graded the exam.   _____ He read the answers carefully.

   (before) _____

3. _____ They were married for five years.   _____ They had a child.

   (when) _____

4. _____ The car collided with a truck.   _____ Someone called the police.

   (after) _____

5. _____ The doctor said she was very healthy.   _____ She was worried.

   (until) _____

6. _____ She slept for ten hours.   _____ I decided to wake her up.

   (by the time) _____

C3 Discussing Previous Accomplishments

▶ Notes 1A, 3A

Work with a partner. Read each situation and look at the picture. Tell what things had been done already and what had not been done yet. Use the expressions in parentheses and the past perfect with *already* and *not … yet.*

1. Sonia was hoping to move into her new apartment a few days early. Yesterday she went to see if it was ready yet.

   (paint the apartment)   *They had already painted the apartment.*

   (clean the carpet)   *They hadn't cleaned the carpet yet.*

   (fix the window)

   (repair the lock)

2. Martin checked to see if he had completed the requirements for graduation.

   (complete the English requirement)

   (take the math courses)

   (pass the writing test)

   Requirements for high school graduation:
   - ✓ 3 Math courses
   - ✓ 4 English courses
   - Writing test

3. Your cousin has been looking for a job for a month. You spoke to her a few days ago.

   (look at the classified ads)

   (go to an employment agency)

   (write her résumé)

HELP WANTED
Attorney for international law firm
Minimum 10 years experience necessary
call 555-6324

EMPLOYMENT AGENCY

Résumé

C4 Describing New Experiences

▶ Notes 1A, 3A

A. These situations describe new experiences. Use the phrases below and the past perfect with *never* and *before* to describe the things that the people had never done before. Then add one of your own ideas.

1. Brian and Jo Ann have just had their first child.

   a. diaper a baby _They had never diapered a baby before._

   b. bathe a baby _____

   c. _____

2. Irina started college last fall.

   a. live on her own _____

   b. sleep in a dormitory _____

   c. _____

3. Dominick got his first summer job at a supermarket.

   a. use an electronic cash register _____

   b. get a paycheck _____

   c. _____

4. Nora took her first driving lesson.

   a. drive a car _____

   b. be so scared _____

   c. _____

B. Think of something you did for the first time. Describe the aspects of the experience that were new to you. Write four sentences using the past perfect and *never*. Then tell your class about your new experience.

New Experience: _I decided to go to Europe for my summer vacation._

1. _I had never flown on a plane before._

2. _____

3. _____

4. _____

The Past Perfect Continuous

Think Critically About Meaning and Use

A. Read the sentences and complete the task below.

_____ **a.** We arrived at 9:30 P.M. Julia had been eating her dinner. (Dinner was just ending.)

_____ **b.** We arrived at 9:30 P.M. Julia had eaten her dinner. (Dinner was over.)

ORGANIZE Match each illustration to the sentence that best describes it.

B. Discuss your answers with the class and read the Meaning and Use Notes to check them.

Meaning and Use Notes

ONLINE
PRACTICE

Order of Events in the Past with Continuing Actions
▶ 1A Similar to the past perfect, the past perfect continuous shows that one action occurred before another action or state in the past. However, the past perfect continuous emphasizes that the first event was ongoing, and continued up to or just before the second event.

Past Perfect Continuous (1st Event)	Simple Past (2nd Event)
Keiko **had been studying** all night.	She **was** exhausted at breakfast.

▶ 1B *For* and *since* show how long a situation lasted before the second past event.

Simple Past (2nd Event)	Past Perfect Continuous (1st Event)
Marie **left** her office at 6:00 P.M.	She**'d been working** <u>since 8:00 A.M.</u>

(Continued on page 136)

▶ **1C** The past perfect continuous is often used in sentences containing past time clauses.

Past Perfect Continuous (1st Event)	**Simple Past (2nd Event)**
Marie **had been working** for nine and a half hours	<u>by the time</u> she **left** her office.

Contrasting the Past Perfect and the Past Perfect Continuous

▶ **2A** Certain common verbs can be used with the past perfect and past perfect continuous with little or no difference in meaning. Remember, though, that using the continuous can show a more intense or emotional situation.

Past Perfect	**Past Perfect Continuous**
Mr. Ortiz **had lived** there since 1960.	Mr. Ortiz **had been living** there since 1960.
I**'d waited** for an hour.	I**'d been waiting** for an hour! I was so angry.

▶ **2B** The past perfect can express a completed action that may or may not have occurred recently. In contrast, the past perfect continuous suggests that an action was continuing up to or ended just before a specific time in the past.

Past Perfect	**Past Perfect Continuous**
Hiro **had watered** the garden before I arrived. (Hiro may have watered it a few minutes or many hours before I arrived.)	Hiro **had been watering** the garden before I arrived. (Hiro watered the garden a few minutes before I arrived.)

 A sentence with the past perfect continuous usually does not tell how many times an action is repeated.

Past Perfect	**Past Perfect Continuous**
I**'d read** it three times before.	**X** I'd been reading it three times before. (INCORRECT)

Adding Background Information to a Sentence

▶ **3** Both the past perfect continuous and the past perfect are often used to provide background information about earlier events. They are used to give reasons with *because* and express contrasts with *although* or *even though*. They are also used to draw conclusions.

Reasons

She looked very tired   <u>because</u> she **had been studying** all night.

<u>because</u> she **had studied** all night.

Contrasts

She looked very tired	<u>although</u> she **had been sleeping** for 12 hours.
	<u>even though</u> she **had slept** for 12 hours.

Conclusions

I realized that	he **had been** criticizing my work.
	he **had** just criticized my work.

D1 Listening for Meaning and Use

▶ Note 2B

CD1 T38 Listen to the two events in each sentence. Check (✓) *Just Before* if the context makes it clear that the first event happened right before the second. Check (✓) *Unclear* if the context does not specify how close together in time the two events were.

	JUST BEFORE	UNCLEAR
1.	✓	
2.		
3.		
4.		
5.		
6.		
7.		
8.		

D2 Talking About Continuing Past Actions

▶ Note 1A–1C

Write two different sentences that tell how long each situation lasted. Use the past perfect continuous with *for* and *since* and simple past time clauses with *when*.

1. Elena worked from 2006 to 2008. Then she went back to school.

   When Elena went back to school, she had been working for two years.
   When Elena went back to school in 2008, she had been working since 2006.

2. Brigitte began to work at C & M in 2009. Her husband joined the company in 2011.

3. The chicken started baking at 5:30. The electricity went off at 5:45.

4. Lisa went to sleep at 11:00 P.M. The phone woke her up at 2:00 A.M.

5. Paulo and Celia got married in 2009. They had their first child in 2011.

6. Kate studied from 2005 to 2011. She graduated from medical school in 2011.

7. Carlos lived in Mexico City from 2008 to 2010. He moved to Paris in 2010.

8. Eric started taking piano lessons in January of 2010. He gave his first recital in July of that year.

D3 Expressing Reasons and Results

▶ Notes 2A, 2B, 3

A. Work with a partner. Complete each sentence with a *because* clause in the past perfect or the past perfect continuous. Then write one more main clause in the simple past and ask your partner to complete it using *because*.

1. He looked very tired _because he had been sleeping poorly._

2. The student was expelled from school _____

3. She quit her job _____

4. _____

B. Now complete each sentence with a main clause in the simple past. Then write one more *because* clause and ask your partner to complete it with a main clause.

1. _He didn't hear the doorbell_____ because he had been listening to music.

2. _____ because we had been exercising.

3. Because she hadn't listened to her parents, _____

4. _____

D4 Expressing Contrasts

▶ Notes 2A, 2B, 3

A. Complete each sentence with a clause using *although* or *even though* in the past perfect or the past perfect continuous.

1. I passed the exam _although I hadn't studied._

2. She was able to answer the question _____

3. _____, everyone became sick.

4. _____, he wanted to quit his job.

B. Complete each sentence with a main clause in the simple past.

1. Even though I had been calling for days, _she never called me back.____

2. _____ although I had gone grocery shopping two days before.

3. Although we had been good friends, _____

4. Even though I had been trying as hard as I could, _____

Beyond the Sentence

Adding Background Information in Longer Discourse

Both the past perfect and the past perfect continuous are often used in a story to give details and background information about an earlier past time. These verb forms usually appear near the beginning of the story. Then the story often continues in the simple past.

> We finally landed in London at 9:30 A.M. We **had been traveling** for thirteen hours and the whole family was exhausted and cranky, especially me. The seat **had been** uncomfortable, and I **hadn't slept** at all. I tried not to be too unpleasant, but it was difficult because nothing seemed to be going right. When we got to the baggage claim area, two suitcases came through quickly, but the other two were missing...

D5 Adding Background Information

A. Read each introductory statement. Then write two or three past perfect or past perfect continuous sentences that provide background information.

1. I was in my favorite restaurant that Sunday afternoon.

We had gathered for a family reunion in honor of my parents' 25th wedding anniversary. My brother and I had been planning this event for months.

2. I remember the day I moved here.

3. I'll never forget that afternoon. We were stuck in heavy traffic on a bridge.

4. I entered my apartment and immediately felt that something was strange.

B. Write a paragraph. Choose one of the items in part A as the beginning of your paragraph. Add some background information in the past perfect or the past perfect continuous. Then complete the paragraph using the simple past to explain more about what happened in the first sentence.

I was in my favorite restaurant that Sunday afternoon. We had gathered for a family reunion in honor of my parents' 25th wedding anniversary. My brother and I had been planning this event for months. We had been emailing each other almost daily with plans, menus, and guest lists. As they had been doing for 25 years, my parents arrived exactly on time. When they saw everyone...

Think Critically About Meaning and Use

A. Read each sentence and the statements that follow. Write *T* if the statement is true, *F* if it is false, or *?* if you do not have enough information to decide.

1. After he had eaten a sandwich, he ate a salad.

    ___F___ **a.** He ate the salad first. Then he ate the sandwich.

    ___F___ **b.** He ate the salad and sandwich together.

2. He had left before the play ended.

    _____ **a.** The play ended. Then he left.

    _____ **b.** He was gone by the end of the play.

3. He had known her for many years when they started to work together.

    _____ **a.** He met her at work.

    _____ **b.** He knew her a long time.

4. Tom didn't lose weight until he went on a diet.

    _____ **a.** Tom didn't lose weight.

    _____ **b.** Tom went on a diet.

5. It was lunchtime. I looked out the window, and I saw that it had rained.

    _____ **a.** It had rained just before I looked out the window.

    _____ **b.** I looked out the window after the rain stopped.

6. He left his job because he had found a better one.

    _____ **a.** He left his job. Then he looked for a better job.

    _____ **b.** He left his job after he found another job.

7. The hospital didn't lose power, although there had been a power failure in the city.

    _____ **a.** The hospital had a power failure.

    _____ **b.** The city lost power.

8. The two men had been working on a project together when I met them.

    _____ **a.** They worked together before I met them.

    _____ **b.** They finished the project.

Edit

Find the errors in these paragraphs and correct them, using either the simple past or the present perfect.

In 1953, Edmund Hillary and Tenzing Norkay ~~had been~~ *were* the first climbers to reach the top of Mount Everest. Since then, many people had climbed Mount Everest, especially in recent years. Before 1953, no human had ever stood on top of the world's highest peak, although some had tried. George Mallory and Sandy Irvine, for example, had died almost 30 years earlier on a perilous path along the North Ridge.

Since 1953, many more people had set world records. In 1975, Junko Tabei of Japan had become the first woman on a mountaineering team to reach the top. In 1980, Reinhold Messner of Italy had become the first person to make the climb to the top alone, without other people and without oxygen. In 1995, Alison Hargreaves of Scotland had duplicated Messner's triumph. She became the first woman to climb Mount Everest solo and without oxygen.

Each climber faces frigid winds, storms, avalanches, and most dangerous of all, the serious effects of the high altitude on the heart, lungs, and brain. So why had many hundreds of people tried to climb Mount Everest in recent years? The only way to explain these numbers is to understand that the climb up Mount Everest represents the ultimate challenge of reaching the "top of the world."

Write

Write an essay about a major event in a famous person's career. Use the past perfect, past perfect continuous, and time clauses to provide background.

1. **BRAINSTORM** Think of a famous person and research his or her life in the library or on the Internet. Decide on the event you will focus on and make a timeline leading up to it. Use these categories to help you organize your ideas into paragraphs.

   - **Introduce the event:** What happened and when?
   - **Discuss background events leading to the event:** What had happened and what had the person been doing before?
   - **Describe and comment on the event:** What happened during the period of the event? What was its significance of the event? How did it affect the rest of the person's career?

2. **WRITE A FIRST DRAFT** Before you write your first draft, read the checklist below and look at the example on page 126. Write your draft using the past perfect and the past perfect continuous.

3. **EDIT** Read your work and check it against the checklist below. Circle grammar, spelling, and punctuation errors.

DO I...	YES
organize my ideas into paragraphs?	☐
use the simple past and past continuous to announce and describe the event?	☐
use the past perfect for completed actions/states that occurred before another past action/state?	☐
use the past perfect continuous for ongoing actions that continued up to or just before another past action/state?	☐
use time clauses and time expressions to clarify the order and duration of past events?	☐

4. **PEER REVIEW** Work with a partner to help you decide how to fix your errors and improve the content. Use the checklist above.

5. **REWRITE YOUR DRAFT** Using the comments from your partner, write a final draft.

> On May 16, 1975, 26-year-old Junko Tabei of Japan became the first woman to reach the top of Mount Everest. Junko had been attracted to mountain climbing since she climbed up Mount Nasu on a school trip at the age of 10. By the time she graduated from university...

Choose the correct word or words to complete each sentence.

1. Where _____ sending her patients for rehabilitation since the nearby facility closed?

   a. has the doctor been   **c.** the doctor has been

   b. the doctor has   **d.** is the doctor

2. Scientists have _____ specimens from the rain forest in order to study their medicinal properties.

   a. take   **b.** took   **c.** taking   **d.** taken

3. The room became quiet when the teacher entered. The students had _____ been talking about her.

   a. yet   **b.** when   **c.** before   **d.** just

4. Why _____ before the end of last year?

   a. unemployment hadn't risen   **c.** hadn't unemployment risen

   b. hasn't unemployment risen   **d.** hasn't unemployment been rising

Choose the correct response to complete each conversation.

5. **A:** I haven't eaten breakfast yet this morning.
   B: _____

       a. Well, there's still time.   **c.** It was delicious, wasn't it?

       b. It's 1:45 P.M. Let's have lunch.   **d.** What about tomorrow?

6. **A:** I've lived in the same apartment for ten years.
   B: _____

       a. Why did you leave it?   **c.** That was a long time ago.

       b. Do you ever feel like moving?   **d.** I hadn't been before.

7. **A:** Your boss has been calling all day.
   B: _____

       a. I'm surprised he called only once.   **c.** I'm glad he hasn't called.

       b. What time did he call?   **d.** How many times did he call?

8. **A:** I've been playing in the same band for eight years.
   B: _____

       a. Why did you quit?   **c.** Are you going to stay with them?

       b. How long ago did you join?   **d.** Had you been together that long?

9. **A:** I've been sleeping late this week.

   B: _____

   a. Had you been going to sleep early?   **c.** Are you going to take a vacation?

   b. Are you on vacation?   **d.** Why haven't you been sleeping?

Reorder each set of words to make a statement or question in the present perfect continuous.

10. jogging/just/you/been/have/?

   _____

11. been/it/long/raining/has/how/?

   _____

Match the response to the statement or question below.

_____ **12.** How long have they been married?   **a.** I haven't seen him for a while.

_____ **13.** Have you taken a vacation lately?   **b.** For about a year.

_____ **14.** When did you last see Jack?   **c.** I'm surprised that they haven't called you.

_____ **15.** We had a long list of things to do. What have we done so far?   **d.** No, but I really need one.

                                                           e. Yes, yesterday.

                                                           f. No, but I hear it's very good.

                                                           g. Well, we've made a lot of progress.

                                                           h. Two years ago.

Complete each sentence with the past perfect form of the words in parentheses. Do not use contractions.

16. After _____ (we/buy) all the ingredients, we made dinner.

17. When the season ended, our team _____ (not/lose) a single game.

Write a question for each response. Use the words in parentheses. Do not use contractions.

18. **A:** (How long) _____

   B: I've been in this room for 30 minutes.

19. **A:** (Where/your sister/lately) _____

   B: She has been on vacation.

20. **A:** (How long) _____

   B: I've been a student for two years.

Modals of Possibility

Doctor Fran's Fitness Forum

A1 Before You Read

Discuss these questions.

What do you and your friends do to stay fit? What benefits can you get from regular exercise? Do you think exercise could be bad for you?

A2 Read

CD1 T39 **Read this post from an online fitness forum to find out about a fitness expert's perspective on the possible dangers of overexercising.**

Doctor Fran's Fitness Forum

TODAY'S TOPIC:

Could Too Much Exercise Hurt You?

Q: Is it possible to exercise too much? My sister runs several marathons a year. She should be the healthiest person I know, but she isn't. Almost every time she takes part in an event,

5   she gets sick with a cold or virus or respiratory infection. I'm starting to think that there might be a link between her training and her illnesses.
Carol *from Portland*

   A: You're right, Carol. Too much exercise could have harmful effects. Your sister may

10   be showing the effects of what the experts call overtraining. All that physical stress on her body might be having a negative effect on her immune system. A recent study of 2,000 runners in the Los Angeles Marathon showed that 13% of the runners became ill the following week. Researchers concluded that marathon runners are six times more likely to get sick after a race and their immune systems may take longer to recover

15   than non-runners. According to experts, moderate exercise should normally strengthen our immune systems but too much exercise could have the opposite effect. It may be hard to believe, but a number of studies on physical education teachers and on former high-school, college, and professional athletes have shown that too much of certain

kinds of exercise might lead to painful and potentially disabling conditions. These, in
20 turn, could result in hip and knee replacements, not to mention broken bones and
years of discomfort.

But, while excessive amounts of exercise and sports may turn out to be bad for you,
most experts agree on one thing. No exercise at all could prove to be even more
harmful in the long run.

▼

---

excessive: more than is necessary or normal
immune system: system of the body that helps you
   fight against infection and disease
in the long run: over a long period of time

moderate: not too much or too little, average
potentially: likely to be or develop in the future
respiratory: of or related to the organs of breathing

A3 After You Read

Choose the answer that best completes each sentence.

1. Carol suspects that her sister's
   frequent illnesses are caused by
   _____.

   a. the environment

   b. her lack of exercise

   c. training

2. Doctor Fran suggests that
   overtraining may have a bad
   effect on _____.

   a. mental readiness

   b. endurance

   c. the immune system

3. Research shows that marathon
   runners often _____ right
   after a race.

   a. have heart attacks

   b. become ill

   c. break bones

4. Moderate exercise normally has
   _____ effect on the
   immune system.

   a. a positive

   b. a negative

   c. no

5. Studies show that, over time, excessive
   exercise can lead to _____ .

   a. bone and joint problems

   b. stronger bones and joints

   c. early retirement

6. Doctor Fran believes that getting
   no exercise is _____
   excessive exercise.

   a. even more harmful than

   b. not as harmful as

   c. equally as harmful as

FORM

Modals of Present and Future Possibility

Think Critically About Form

A. Look back at the article on page 146 and complete the tasks below.

1. IDENTIFY Look at the three underlined examples of modals of present and future possbility. Find six more examples.

2. CATEGORIZE Sort your examples into modals followed by:

a. *be*   b. *be* + verb + *-ing*   c. a different main verb

B. Discuss your answers with the class and read the Form charts to check them.

▶ Present Modals

ONLINE
PRACTICE

AFFIRMATIVE STATEMENTS			
SUBJECT	**MODAL**	**MAIN VERB OR *BE* (+ VERB + -*ING*)**	
He	**may** / **might**	**have**	a car.
She	**could**	**be meeting**	him now.
They	**should** / **must**	**be**	home.

NEGATIVE STATEMENTS			
SUBJECT	**MODAL + *NOT***	**MAIN VERB OR *BE* (+ VERB + -*ING*)**	
He	**may not** / **might not**	**have**	a car.
She	**couldn't** / **can't**	**be meeting**	him now.
They	**shouldn't** / **must not**	**be**	home.

▶ Future Modals

AFFIRMATIVE STATEMENTS			
SUBJECT	**MODAL**	**MAIN VERB OR *BE* (+ VERB + -*ING*)**	
He	**may** / **might**	**get**	a car soon.
She	**could**	**be meeting**	him later.
They	**should** / **will**	**be**	home soon.

NEGATIVE STATEMENTS			
SUBJECT	**MODAL + *NOT***	**MAIN VERB OR *BE* (+ VERB + -*ING*)**	
He	**may not** / **might not**	**get**	a car soon.
She	**couldn't** / **can't**	**be meeting**	him later.
They	**shouldn't** / **won't**	**be**	home yet.

Modals of Present Possibility

- Modals have only one form with all subjects.

- *Must not*, *may not*, and *might not* have no contracted forms as modals of possibility.

 Do not confuse the two words *may be* (modal + *be*) with *maybe*, a one-word adverb that often begins a sentence.

He **may be** late.   **Maybe** he's late.

- *Could* and *can* are used to ask questions about present possibility. *Might* is very uncommon. Use *be* in short answers to questions containing *be*.

  A: **Could** he **be sleeping**?   A: **Can** it **be true**?

  B: He **might be**.   B: It **must not be**.

- See Appendix 14 for contractions with *should*, *could*, and *can*.

Modals of Future Possibility

- *Must (not)*, *can't*, and *couldn't* are not usually used to express future possibility unless they are combined with the continuous.

  She **must not be getting** a new car next month.

- *Could* may be used to ask questions about future possibility. Notice the short answers.

  A: **Could** he **arrive** before we get home?   B: Yes, he **might**. / No, he **won't**.

- See Appendix 14 for contractions with *will*.

▶ Present Phrasal Modals

AFFIRMATIVE STATEMENTS

SUBJECT	MODAL	MAIN VERB OR *BE* (+ VERB + -*ING*)	
He	**ought to**	**be**	home.
She	**has to** **has got to**	**be riding**	her bike.
They	**have to** **have got to**	**have**	a car.

CONTRACTIONS

She**'s** They**'ve**	**got to**	**have**	a car.

▶ Future Phrasal Modals

AFFIRMATIVE STATEMENTS

SUBJECT	MODAL	MAIN VERB OR *BE* (+ VERB + -*ING*)	
He	**ought to**	**be**	
She	**has to** **has got to**	**be coming**	home soon.
They	**have to** **have got to**		

CONTRACTIONS

She**'s** They**'ve**	**got to**	**to be coming**	home soon.

(Continued on page 150)

Phrasal Modals of Present Possibility

• The phrasal modal *ought to* has one form with all subjects. The phrasal modals *have to* and *have got to* have different third-person singular forms.

• None of these phrasal modals is used in the negative to express possibility.

• *Have got to* has contracted forms. *Ought to* and *have to* do not.

Phrasal Modals of Future Possibility

• *Have to* and *have got to* are only used to express future possibility with the continuous.

  They**'ve got to be arriving** soon.

B1 Listening for Form

CD1 T40 **Listen to this story and write the modals or phrasal modals you hear. Use contractions if you hear them.**

The Abominable Snowman of the Himalayas and the Loch Ness Monster of Scotland are two creatures that _____ may _____ or

_____ may not _____ be real—that depends

on your beliefs. If you ask someone about them,

they _____³_____ respond, "That

_____⁴_____ be true," or they

_____⁵_____ respond, "That

_____⁶_____ be true." Over the years,

it has been difficult to separate fact from fiction

as stories about these creatures continue.

The Loch Ness Monster or a hoax?

_____⁷_____ it be true that an ape-like creature with long hair lives high

in the Himalayas? _____⁸_____ the large footprints found there belong to

such a creature? While many scientists say this _____⁹_____ be a myth, others

claim that there _____¹⁰_____ be some kind of creature out there. But no one

knows for sure.

In Scotland, _____ there really be a mysterious water monster
                        11

with a long neck and a large body like a brontosaurus? Many claim that there

_____ be some truth to this story that's been around since the fifteenth
          12

century. Just ask the two million tourists who visit the area each year, hoping to see

the monster.

B2 Completing Conversations with Modals

**Work with a partner. Complete the conversations with the words in parentheses.
Use contractions when possible. Then practice the conversations.**

Conversation 1

A: That number _____ *may not be* _____ (be/not/may) right.
                         1

B: Don't worry. It _____ (be/not/can) wrong. The computer doesn't
                              2

make mistakes!

Conversation 2

A: They _____ (arrive/should) soon.
                    1

B: I doubt it. They probably _____ (arrive/not/will) until later.
                                        2

A: No, I spoke to them a half hour ago. They _____ (be/ought to) here
                                                          3

in 20 minutes.

Conversation 3

A: This _____ (be/have to) a mistake. My phone bill
                    1

_____ (be/not/could) $300 for just one month!
          2

B: Don't worry about it. Just call up the phone company. There _____
                                                                              3

(be/must) an explanation.

Conversation 4

A: Why isn't Sasha home yet? The movie _____ (be/have got to)
                                                     1

over by now.

B: Actually, it just ended. He _____ (be/should) here soon.
                                          2

B3 Using Short Answers with Modals

Work with a partner. Switch roles for each question.

Student A: Ask a question about healthy living.

Student B: Answer the question with your beliefs. Use positive or negative short answers with *may, might, must,* or *could.* Use *be* where necessary.

1. Do carrots improve your eyesight?

   A: Do carrots improve your eyesight?

   B: They may. OR *They may not.*

2. Is moderate exercise good for everyone?

   A: Is moderate exercise good for everyone?

   B: It must be. OR *It couldn't be.*

3. Do eggs cause heart disease?

4. Is coffee good for your memory?

5. Do cell phones cause cancer?

6. Are microwave ovens bad for you?

7. Does table salt lower your blood pressure?

8. Are full-time jobs bad for you?

B4 Building Sentences with Modals

Build as many meaningful sentences as possible. Use an item from each column. Punctuate your sentences correctly.

John must be sleeping.

John it	must might can't has to	be have	sleeping true a problem broken

B5 Writing Your Own Sentences with Modals

Think about a distant city where you have relatives or friends. Use modals of present possibility to do the tasks below.

1. Write three sentences about the weather in the city you are thinking about.

   It must be raining in Rio.

   It may be cool…

2. Write three sentences describing what you think your friends or relatives are doing right now.

   Carla must be traveling.

   Marco might be teaching a class, or he could be…

Modals of Present Possibility

Think Critically About Meaning and Use

A. Read the sentences and answer the questions below.

a. He must be telling the truth. He never lies.
b. He may be telling the truth. I'm not sure.
c. He can't be telling the truth. His story doesn't make sense.
d. He could be telling the truth. It's possible, I guess.
e. He might be telling the truth. I don't know.
f. He should be telling the truth. He usually does.

1. ANALYZE In which sentences is the speaker more certain?

2. ANALYZE In which sentences is the speaker less certain?

B. Discuss your answers with the class and read the Meaning and Use Notes to check them.

Meaning and Use Notes

ONLINE PRACTICE

	Overview

▶ **1** Modals and phrasal modals of possibility are used to express guesses, expectations, or inferences about present situations. The modal you choose shows how certain you are that something is true.

Less Certain	• could, might, might not	Jim **could be** upstairs, or he **might be** outside.
	• may, may not	He **may not be** awake yet. I'm not sure.
	• should, shouldn't, ought to	Jim **should be** upstairs. I saw him go up a few minutes ago.
	• must, must not, have to, have got to	I don't see Jim. He **must not be feeling** well. He **has to be** upstairs.
More Certain	• can't, couldn't	Jim **couldn't be** upstairs. I saw him go out.

(Continued on page 154)

Guessing with *Could*, *Might*, and *May*

▶ **2** Use *could*, *might (not)*, and *may (not)* to guess about a present situation when you don't have much proof. *Could* and *might* sometimes show less certainty than *may*, especially when they express more than one possibility.

More Certain

A: Where's Jim?

B: He **may be** upstairs.

Less Certain

A: Where's Jim?

B: He **could be** upstairs, or he **might be** outside.

Expectations with *Should* and *Ought To*

▶ **3** Use *should(n't)* and *ought to* when you have an expectation about a present situation based on proof or experience.

A: Where's Jim?

B: He **should be** upstairs. I saw him go up a few minutes ago.

Expectations expressed with *should* and *ought to* may be confused with the meanings of advisability and necessity that are also expressed by these modals. To make the meaning clear, the context must be stated or understood.

Jim **ought to be** in bed. I thought I saw him go upstairs before. (*ought to* = expectation)

Jim **ought to be** in bed. He looks very sick. (*ought to* = advisability)

Strong Certainty and Understanding with *Must*, *Have To*, and *Have Got To*

▶ **4A** Use *must (not)*, *have to*, and *have got to* to draw conclusions when you are certain of something, and you believe there is only one logical explanation.

A: We can't find Jim.

B: He ⎧ must ⎫ be upstairs. We've looked everywhere else.
      ⎨ has to ⎬
      ⎩ has got to ⎭

▶ **4B** In conversation, *must be* or *must feel* with an adjective often show understanding of someone's feelings.

A: I hardly slept at all last night. My neighbors had a party.

B: You **must be** very annoyed at them.

C: You **must feel** tired. Do you still want to go out later?

Strong Certainty with *Can't* and *Couldn't*

▶ **5A**	Use *can't* and *couldn't* when you are certain something is unlikely or impossible. Notice that in the affirmative, however, *could* expresses less certainty. A: I think Jim is upstairs. B: He **couldn't be** upstairs. I saw him go out. (*couldn't* = strong certainty) A: Well, I **could be** wrong. (*could* = less certainty)
▶ **5B**	*Can't* and *couldn't* sometimes express surprise or disbelief. A: I heard that you're going to be promoted. B: That **can't be** true. The boss doesn't like me. (*can't* = disbelief)

C1 Listening for Meaning and Use

▶ Notes 1–3, 4A, 4B, 5A, 5B

CD1 T41 Listen to each situation. Is the speaker expressing less certainty or more certainty about the situation? Check (✓) the correct column.

	LESS CERTAINTY	MORE CERTAINTY
1.	✓	
2.		
3.		
4.		
5.		
6.		
7.		
8.		

C2 Expressing Degrees of Certainty

▶ Notes 1–3, 4A

Work with a partner. Read each question and the two responses. Then complete each response with a modal that expresses the appropriate degree of certainty. More than one answer may be possible for each item.

Conversation 1

A: What's wrong with Alice? She has been looking strange ever since class ended.

B: She ___*might*___ be upset. I don't think she did very well on the exam.
   1

C: She ___*must*___ be upset. I saw her exam. She got a very low grade.
   2

Conversation 2

A: Are the clothes dry yet?

B: They _____ be dry by now. They usually take 45 minutes to dry, and they've
   1
been in the dryer almost 40 minutes.

C: They _____ be dry by now. They usually take 45 minutes, and they've been in
   2
the dryer for almost an hour.

Conversation 3

A: Do you think they've finished repairing your car by now?

B: It _____ be ready. It's 2:00 P.M., and they said it'd be ready at noon.
   1

C: It _____ be ready. It's noon. They said it would probably be ready by noon.
   2

Conversation 4

A: Whose black jacket is this? Someone forgot to take it after the meeting.

B: It _____ be Diane's. I saw her wearing a black jacket earlier.
   1

C: It _____ be Diane's. She wears a lot of black.
   2

Conversation 5

A: It's 10:30 P.M. Who could be calling so late?

B: It _____ be Chris. She said she wanted to talk to me today.
   1

C: It _____ be Chris. She said she was going to call after ten o'clock.
   2

C3 Guessing with *Could, Might,* and *May*

▶ Note 2

Work in small groups. Describe what you think the people in the pictures are doing. Use *could*, *might*, and *may* to make as many guesses as you can.

They could be watching a car show.
They might be looking at…

C4 Making Guesses and Drawing Conclusions

▶ Notes 1, 2, 4A

Work in small groups. Write guesses and conclusions about each situation below. Use *could*, *must*, *may*, *might*, *has to*, and *has got to*. Add one or two more sentences to explain what you mean. Discuss your answers.

1. The teacher is absent today.

   She must be sick. She wasn't feeling well yesterday. OR
   She might be out of town, or she could be sick. Nobody knows. OR
   She might not be feeling well again. She was sick a few weeks ago.

2. The fire alarm is ringing.

3. Your new neighbor never smiles.

4. Everyone's eating chocolate cake for dessert except Tina.

5. You've been sneezing all morning.

6. Your sister has just received a dozen long-stemmed roses with no card.

7. Jenny isn't answering the telephone.

8. Sam always looks tired.

C5 Stating Expectations and Drawing Conclusions ▶ Notes 3, 4A

Work with a partner. Terry is a nurse. Read Terry's work schedule and complete each sentence below. Give your conclusions or expectations using *must be* or *should be* + a continuous verb or a time of day.

Day Shift Schedule	
6:45 A.M.	meet with night nurses
7:15 A.M.	check vital signs of patients (temperature, pulse, blood pressure)
7:45 A.M.	meet with doctors
8:30 A.M.	give patients medicine
10:00 A.M.	write notes on charts
11:00 A.M.	discharge patients
12:30 P.M.	attend meeting
1:00 P.M.	admit new patients
2:45 P.M.	take a break
4:30 P.M.	go home

1. If it's 7:20, *Terry must be checking the patients' vital signs.*

    OR *Terry should be checking the patients' vital signs.*

2. If Terry is meeting with the doctors, *it must be 7:45.*   OR *it should be 7:45.*

3. If it's 1:10, _____

4. If Terry is going home, _____

5. If it's 8:30, _____

6. If it's 11:00, _____

7. If it's 6:50, _____

8. If Terry is writing notes on charts, _____

9. If Terry is taking a break, _____

10. If it's 12:30, _____

C6 Expressing Understanding

▶ Note 4B

Work with a partner. Take turns reading these statements. Answer with *you must be* or *you must feel* + an adjective to show your understanding of each situation.

1. I studied all night for my exam.

   You must be exhausted. OR *You must feel tired.*

2. I didn't eat breakfast or lunch today.

3. Tomorrow is my first job interview.

4. My English teacher canceled our midterm exam.

5. My friends are going to visit me next week. I haven't seen them for six months.

6. My car broke down again. I just spent $300 on it last week.

7. I didn't get accepted to graduate school.

8. My parents are going to go on a cruise next month.

C7 Expressing Strong Certainty and Disbelief

▶ Notes 4A, 4B, 5A, 5B

A. Work with a partner. Write a dialogue in which the speakers express strong certainty and surprise or disbelief about one of the topics below. Use some of these modals: *can't, couldn't, must, have to, have got to.*

1. A young person is trying to make excuses to his or her parents about not doing well in school.

   Young person: *There's got to be a mistake. My grades can't be that bad.*

   Parent: *You must be kidding! What about the homework that you didn't do, and the classes that you missed?*

   Young person: *Well,…*

2. Two friends are discussing the surprising behavior of a mutual friend.

3. Two co-workers are discussing some rumors that are going around the office.

4. Two teachers are discussing a student's work, which has suddenly improved.

B. Practice your dialogue. Be prepared to present it to the class.

D | MEANING AND USE 2

Modals of Future Possibility

Think Critically About Meaning and Use

A. Read the sentences and answer the questions below.

   a. The plane might be on time. It's not clear yet.
   b. The plane should be on time. It left on time.
   c. The plane could be on time. They sometimes make up time in the air.
   d. The plane will be on time. They just announced it.

   1. ANALYZE In which sentences is the speaker less certain?

   2. ANALYZE In which sentences is the speaker more certain?

   3. INTERPRET Which sentences have about the same meaning?

B. Discuss your answers with the class and read the Meaning and Use Notes to check them.

Meaning and Use Notes

ONLINE PRACTICE

	Overview
▶ 1	Modals and phrasal modals of possibility are used to make predictions about the future. The modal you choose can make your sentence sound more or less certain.

Less Certain	• could, might, might not	The plane **could arrive** soon.
↕	• may, may not	The plane **may arrive** soon.
	• should, shouldn't, ought to	The plane **should arrive** soon.
More Certain	• will, won't	The plane **will arrive** soon.

> ❗ *Must (not), can't, couldn't, have to,* and *have got to* are not usually used to express beliefs about the future unless they are combined with the continuous. They are used to express certainty about the present.
>
> They **must be coming** home soon.
>
> ✗ They must not be home later. (INCORRECT)

Guessing with *Could*, *Might*, and *May*

▶ **2**   Use *could*, *might (not)*, and *may (not)* to guess about a future situation when you don't have much proof. *Could* and *might* sometimes show less certainty than *may*, especially when they are used to express more than one possibility.

More Certain	**Less Certain**
A: When is Liz arriving?	A: When is Liz arriving?
B: She **may be arriving** soon.	B: She **could arrive** at 7:30, but she **might be** late.

Expectations with *Should* and *Ought To*

▶ **3**   Use *should(n't)* and *ought to* when you have an expectation about a future situation based on proof or experience. *Should* and *ought to* are used to indicate future expectations more frequently than present expectations.

A: When is she coming?

B: She **should be** here at 7:30. That's what she told me yesterday.

> Expectations expressed by *should* and *ought to* can become confused with the meanings of advisability and necessity that are also expressed by these modals. To make the meaning clear, the context must be stated or understood.
>
> Liz **ought to be** here on Monday. She said she's coming. (*ought to* = possibility)
>
> Liz **ought to be** here on Monday. I told her to come. (*ought to* = advisability)

Strong Certainty with *Will* and *Won't*

▶ **4A**   Use *will* and *won't* to express strong certainty about the future.

She**'ll come** soon. I'm not worried. (very likely)

She **won't be coming**. (very unlikely)

▶ **4B**   *Will* is often weakened with adverbs of possibility such as *maybe*, *perhaps*, and *probably*. *Probably* is the strongest of these adverbs, although it still expresses a small amount of doubt.

Maybe she**'ll come**. (= She **might come**.)

Perhaps she**'ll come**. (= She **might come**.)

She**'ll probably come**. (= She **should be coming**.)

D1 Listening for Meaning and Use

▶ Notes 1–3, 4A, 4B

🔊 CD1 T42 Listen to each situation. Is the speaker expressing less certainty or more certainty about the future situation? Check (✓) the correct column.

	LESS CERTAINTY	MORE CERTAINTY
1.	✓	
2.		
3.		
4.		
5.		
6.		
7.		
8.		

D2 Expressing Degrees of Certainty

▶ Notes 1–3, 4A, 4B

Rewrite each sentence using a modal to express the appropriate degree of certainty about the future. More than one answer may be possible for each item.

1. I expect the exam to be easy.

   The exam should be easy.

2. Maybe we'll come later.

3. The flight definitely arrives at 8:10.

4. There's a small chance of rain this afternoon.

5. I don't expect it to be cold tonight.

6. There's a good possibility that he'll get the job.

7. It's possible that video exercise games will become more challenging.

8. Perhaps he's taking the express train this evening.

9. I'm certain that the class meets on Thursdays next semester.

10. She's probably in Miami for the winter.

D3 Making Predictions About the Weather

▶ Notes 1–3, 4A, 4B

Work in small groups. Look at the four-day weather forecast and describe the weather for each day. Use affirmative or negative modals, and adverbs of possibility.

TONIGHT

High	Low
34°F	30°F

Travel advisory: definite snowfall, heavy at times, and 5 to 8 inches expected by tomorrow morning.

1. <u>There will be heavy snow tonight. We should have five to eight inches by morning.</u> OR <u>There will probably be five to eight inches by morning.</u>

SATURDAY

High	Low
40°F	35°F

80% chance of rain accompanied by strong winds. Partial cleaning in the afternoon, but returning clouds in the evening with a 50% chance of rain. Possibility of flooding.

3. _____

TOMORROW

High	Low
38°F	32°F

Increasing chance of clouds, 30% chance of sleet in the afternoon. Rain likely overnight.

2. _____

SUNDAY

High	Low
45°F	39°F

Sunshine followed by partly cloudy skies late in the afternoon. A slight chance of snow in the evening. Thickening clouds, but snow very unlikely after midnight.

4. _____

D4 Making Predictions About Your Lifetime

▶ Notes 1–3, 4A, 4B

A. Complete each sentence with an affirmative or negative modal to make a prediction about your lifetime.

1. During my lifetime, more people _____will_____ live to the age of 100.

2. People _____may not_____ visit other planets.

3. Researchers _____ find a cure for cancer.

4. Astronomers _____ solve the mysteries of the universe.

5. People _____ live on Mars.

6. I _____ ride in a spaceship.

7. Robots _____ do all of our housework.

8. Countries _____ stop producing nuclear weapons.

9. Scientists _____ find ways to predict earthquakes.

10. There _____ be another world war.

B. Now write five more predictions about things that *could*, *might*, *may*, or *will* happen in your lifetime. Use adverbs of possibility in at least two of your sentences.

In the future, robots may assist the elderly with all of their household chores.

Maybe everyone will be driving electric cars.

My country will probably host the Olympics.

C. Follow these steps to write a paragraph about one of your predictions from parts A or B.

1. Write down some details about the prediction.

2. Use the prediction to write a clear introductory sentence and a paragraph explaining what might or might not happen.

3. Make sure to use various modals and adverbs of possibility, but don't use them in every sentence.

   During my lifetime, people may not visit other planets, but unmanned space vehicles will certainly continue to visit them. People might be able to…

Think Critically About Meaning and Use

A. Work with a partner. Read each situation. Choose the sentence that is the most certain.

1. The key is missing.
   a. It may be on the table.
   b. It must be on the table.
   c. It ought to be on the table.

2. A letter has just arrived.
   a. It can't be from Mary.
   b. It must not be from Mary.
   c. It might not be from Mary.

3. Thomas is doing his homework.
   a. He might finish by four o'clock.
   b. He could finish by four o'clock.
   c. He won't finish by four o'clock.

4. The answer is 25.
   a. That may not be right.
   b. That couldn't be right.
   c. That might not be right.

5. The doorbell is ringing.
   a. It has to be the mail carrier.
   b. It should be the mail carrier.
   c. It ought to be the mail carrier.

6. My car is at the service station.
   a. It won't be ready soon.
   b. It will probably be ready soon.
   c. It ought to be ready soon.

B. Discuss these questions in small groups.

1. **GENERATE** Look at sentence 1. Imagine you know for sure that the key is <u>not</u> on the table. What two modal forms could you use to replace *must be*?

2. **PREDICT** Look at sentence 6a. What might the speaker say next to support the idea?

Edit

Find the errors in this paragraph and correct them.

A migraine is a severe headache that can ~~to~~ affect your quality of life. Migraine sufferers often experience symptoms such as zigzag flashing lights or blind spots in their vision. However, there are other symptoms that could signaling that a migraine is coming. You maybe sensitive to light, sound, or smells, or you might be feel overly tired. The good news is that treatment must often relieve the pain and symptoms and prevent further attacks.

Write

Imagine that you are the health editor of your school's online newspaper. Write an article discussing ways that students might stay fit while they are studying at your school. Use modals and phrasal modals of present and future possibility.

1. **BRAINSTORM** Think about all the problems that students face and the solutions that you might include. Use these categories to help you organize your ideas into three or four paragraphs.

   • **Problems:** Why might students find it difficult to stay fit while they are studying (e.g., sitting for too many hours, study/sleep habits, food)?
   • **Solutions/Advice:** What are some of the things that students might do to stay fit (e.g., exercise, eat properly, get enough sleep)?
   • **Conclusion:** What may happen if they don't follow your advice? What benefits might they experience if they follow your suggestions?

2. **WRITE A FIRST DRAFT** Before you write your first draft, read the checklist below and look at the examples on pages 146–147. Write your draft using modals of possibility.

3. **EDIT** Read your work and check it against the checklist below. Circle grammar, spelling, and punctuation errors.

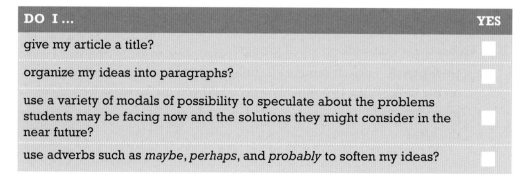

DO I ...	YES
give my article a title?	☐
organize my ideas into paragraphs?	☐
use a variety of modals of possibility to speculate about the problems students may be facing now and the solutions they might consider in the near future?	☐
use adverbs such as *maybe*, *perhaps*, and *probably* to soften my ideas?	☐

4. **PEER REVIEW** Work with a partner to help you decide how to fix your errors and improve the content. Use the checklist above.

5. **REWRITE YOUR DRAFT** Using the comments from your partner, write a final draft.

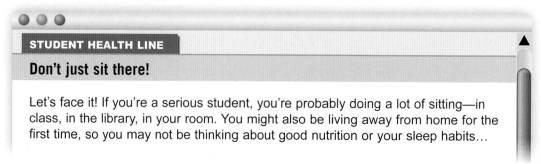

STUDENT HEALTH LINE

Don't just sit there!

Let's face it! If you're a serious student, you're probably doing a lot of sitting—in class, in the library, in your room. You might also be living away from home for the first time, so you may not be thinking about good nutrition or your sleep habits...

Past Modals

The Really Early Birds

A1 Before You Read

Discuss these questions.

Have you ever thought about how birds are able to fly? Do you know what makes it possible? Have you ever dreamed or wished you could fly?

A2 Read

 CD1 T43 **Read this magazine article to find out what new evidence has been found about how birds first learned to fly.**

The Really Early Birds

A new theory explains how the first feathered creatures to fly <u>may have gotten</u> off the ground. Researchers believe that a prehistoric
5 bird that descended from dinosaurs, archaeopteryx (pronounced "ar-kee-op-te-riks"), had a good wingspan for a half-pound bird—more than 20 inches. That has to have been enough
10 to enable the crow-sized bird to fly, or at least glide, through the Jurassic skies. But the toughest part of flying is the takeoff. And the first birds and their dinosaur ancestors just didn't
15 have the same specialized muscle power for liftoff that their modern descendants do. It's a question that scientists have been arguing about for

more than 200 years. How did the
20 first fliers get into the air? A study in the journal Nature shows how it could have happened.

Fly or die? According to this popular theory, a tree-dwelling
25 prehistoric bird could have launched itself—or could have fallen—from its perch and managed to stay up by flapping its wings. That solves the gravity issue, but Luis Chiappe, a
30 palaeontologist at the Natural History Museum of Los Angeles County, points out a problem. "We don't know of any bird ancestors that lived in trees."

35 **A running start?** This could have helped a bird like archaeopteryx into

the air, but the ancient bird's estimated speed wasn't fast enough for liftoff. Chiappe worked with an expert in aerodynamics, Phillip Burgers, to simulate the takeoff of the archaeopteryx. They found that the bird's wings were able to rotate in a way that may have provided the extra burst of speed needed to outrun a hungry predator or catch a quick-running lizard. And, the new calculations show, the wing flapping could have generated sufficient speed for takeoff. During the early phase of liftoff, archaeopteryx's wings must have acted more like an airplane's engines, providing extra speed. Then, when the archaeopteryx was in the air, it must have rotated its wings back to horizontal position, to maintain altitude.

Modern birds do exactly the same thing, so why hasn't anyone noticed until now? Experts have been fascinated by lift, probably because it's something humans can't do. Chiappe and Burgers have shown that the archaeopteryx could have taken off from the ground, but whether or not it actually did may never be known. According to the researchers, the answer to this question is not really important. Rather, the importance of their discovery is that the wings could have helped the archaeopteryx gain speed. Flying might have developed as the archaeopteryx ran faster and faster while flapping its wings, not by falling out of trees. Perhaps flying is just the continuation of running by other means.

Adapted from *Newsweek*

---

aerodynamics: the science that studies forces that act on things moving through air

altitude: height in the air

Jurassic: the time period when dinosaurs and the earliest birds lived

paleontologist: a scientist who studies fossils to learn about the history of life on earth

predator: an animal that lives by killing and eating other animals

wingspan: measurement across the wings when the wings are extended

A3 After You Read

Check (✓) the facts that scientists who study prehistoric birds are certain about.

_✓_ **1.** They had feathers.

_____ **2.** They descended from dinosaurs.

_____ **3.** They had wings.

_____ **4.** They were much smaller than modern birds.

_____ **5.** They could fly.

_____ **6.** They lived in trees.

B FORM

Past Modals

Think Critically About Form

A. Look back at the article on page 168 and complete the tasks below.

1. **IDENTIFY** An example of a past modal is underlined. Find six more examples.

2. **COMPARE AND CONTRAST** Find two past modals with singular subjects and two with plural subjects. Is there any difference in form between them?

3. **EVALUATE** What auxiliary follows the modals? What is the form of the main verbs?

B. Discuss your answers with the class and read the Form charts to check them.

▶ Past Modals

ONLINE
PRACTICE

AFFIRMATIVE STATEMENTS				
SUBJECT	MODAL	*HAVE*	PAST PARTICIPLE	
I	may might could should must	have	passed	the test.

NEGATIVE STATEMENTS				
SUBJECT	MODAL + NOT	*HAVE*	PAST PARTICIPLE	
I	may not might not couldn't can't shouldn't must not	have	passed	the test.

- Past modals have only one form with all subjects.

- Past modals have two auxiliary verbs: a modal and *have*. Only the modal forms contractions.

- *May not have*, *might not have*, and *must not have* have no contracted forms as past modals.

- *Could have* and *should have* may be used to ask questions with past modals. Notice that short answers contain modal + *have* and optional main verb *be* if appropriate.

  A: **Could** they **have called**?   A: **Should** she **have been** at the meeting?

  B: No, they **must not have**.   B: Yes, she **should have been**.

- See Appendix 14 for contractions with *can*, *could*, and *should*.

- See Appendix 6 for irregular verbs and their past participles.

▶ Past Phrasal Modals

AFFIRMATIVE STATEMENTS			
SUBJECT	MODAL	*HAVE*	PAST PARTICIPLE
He	**ought to**	**have**	**come**.
She	**has to** **has got to**	**have**	**known**.
You	**have to** **have got to**		

NEGATIVE STATEMENTS			
SUBJECT	MODAL + NOT	*HAVE*	PAST PARTICIPLE
He	**ought not to**	**have**	**come**.

CONTRACTIONS			
She**'s** You**'ve**	got to	have	known.

- *Ought to have* has only one form. *Have to have* and *have got to have* have different third-person singular forms.
- *Ought to have* can be used in the affirmative or negative. *Have to have* and *have got to have* are used only in the affirmative.
- *Have got to have* has contracted forms. *Have to have* and *ought to have* do not.
- *Had to have* + past participle can often replace *have to have* + past participle.

You { **have to have** / **had to have** } known the answer.

B1 Listening for Form

Listen to this podcast and write the past modals you hear.

Most scientists now agree that an asteroid collision or a similar event ____must have____ been responsible for
1
starting the mass extinction of dinosaurs and other animals about 65 million years ago. But there is still disagreement about another wave of extinction that occurred more recently, just 13,000 years ago. That's when great woolly mammoths, mastodons, saber-tooth tigers, and other large animals known as megafauna died off in northern Eurasia and the Americas.

What _____ caused the disappearance of these great beasts? Some
2
say that human colonizers from Siberia _____ done the damage over a
3
period of a thousand years. But others disagree. In their opinion, a relatively small group of hunters _____ killed off so many animals across three whole
4
continents. As one researcher told me, "We _____ found evidence of
5
such overhunting, but we haven't. So humans _____ been the cause."
6

Others think it _____ been climate change. Scientists know that
7
there was a cold snap that led to a partial return to Ice Age conditions between 12,900 and 11,500 years ago, and some believe that this _____ put stress on
8
the megafauna. Again, for the theory to be true, they _____ found
9
proof, but so far they haven't.

The most recent theory is that a major cosmic catastrophe such as an airburst or impact from a comet _____ caused the extinctions. Evidence to
10
support this _____ already been found in soil samples at more than
11
50 sites across North America, and glacier scientists think they _____
12
found signs in the Greenland ice sheet as well.

B2 Completing Conversations

 Work with a partner. Complete these conversations using the past modal form of the words in parentheses. Then practice the conversations using contractions where appropriate.

Conversation 1

A: I ___could have gone___ (could/go) to the movies with you, but I decided to
    1
study instead.

B: You didn't miss anything. You _____ (might/not/like) it anyway.
    2
There _____ (must/be) ten different violent scenes!
    3

Conversation 2

A: I _____ (should/not/drive) to work this morning. There was so
    1
much traffic.

B: You _____ (should/take) the bus. It was empty.
    2

Conversation 3

A: She _____ (could/not/leave) yet. We're not that late.
    1

B: But she _____ (might/forget) to wait for us.
    2

Conversation 4

A: You _____ (must/not/got) much sleep last night.
    1

B: You're right. I was up coughing and sneezing most of the night. I

_____ (should/go) to the doctor yesterday, He _____
    2   3
(could/write) me a prescription for some cold medicine.

Conversation 5

A: I lost my keys last night. I _____ (might/leave) them at your house.
    1

B: No, you _____ (could/not). You drove home with them.
    2

A: That's right. Then I _____ (must/drop) them after I parked the car.
    3

B: You _____ (might/lock) them in your car. Have you checked?
    4

B3 Asking and Answering Questions with Past Modals

 Work with a partner. Switch roles for each question.

Student A: Ask a question about prehistoric birds. Use the words below with *could have.*

Student B: Answer the question in your own opinion. Use short answers with modals.

1. have feathers

   A: *Could prehistoric birds have had feathers?*
   B: *Yes, they could have.* OR *They must have.*

2. descend from dinosaurs

   A: *Could prehistoric birds have descended from dinosaurs?*
   B: *No, they couldn't have.*

3. have wings

4. jump from trees

5. run fast

6. live on the ground

7. eat smaller animals

8. eat seeds

B4 Forming Past Modals

Rewrite these sentences. Change the modals to past modals.

1. The researchers might be wrong. There may be some data they ignored.

   The researchers might have been wrong. There may have been some data they ignored.

2. The report should be available on April 12.

3. He ought to study more for the test.

4. I could work harder.

5. She has to be home.

6. I should do things differently. I should exercise more. I know I could find the time.

7. I should relax more. Perhaps I could learn yoga.

8. I shouldn't worry so much. Worrying couldn't be good for my health.

Informally Speaking

Reducing Past Modals

CD1 T45 Look at the cartoon and listen to the conversation. How is each underlined form in the cartoon different from what you hear?

This traffic is terrible. We <u>should have</u> stayed in the office!

Yeah. We <u>could have</u> left after rush hour.

In informal speech, affirmative and negative past modals are often reduced. Have may sound like /əv/. If it is reduced even more, it sounds like /ə/.

Standard Form	What You Might Hear		
I **could have** come.	"I /ˈkʊdəv/ come."	OR	"I /ˈkʊdə/ come."
They **must have** come.	"They /ˈmʌstəv/ come."	OR	"They /ˈmʌstə/ come."
He **may not have** come.	"He /ˈmeɪnɑtəv/ come."	OR	"He /ˈmeɪnɑdə/ come."
We **should not have** come.	"We /ˈʃʊdntəv/ come."	OR	"We /ˈʃʊdndə/ come."

B5 Understanding Informal Speech

CD1 T46 Listen and write the standard form of the words you hear.

A: I'm sorry I'm late. I _____*should have*_____ called you. Then you

_____(2)_____ met me downtown.

B: That _____(3)_____ worked anyway. I didn't get out of work until six.

And then there _____(4)_____ been fifty people waiting for the elevator.

It took me ten minutes to get out of the building.

A: So where's Linda? She _____(5)_____ been here by now. She

_____(6)_____ forgotten.

B: I doubt that. She _____(7)_____ gotten stuck in traffic, or she

_____(8)_____ left work late, too. Let's sit down over there and wait for her.

Modals of Past Possibility

Think Critically About Meaning and Use

A. Read the sentences and answer the questions below.

a. Prehistoric birds must have been able to fly. They had wings.
b. Prehistoric birds could have been able to fly. They were small.
c. Prehistoric birds might have been able to fly. They were light enough.
d. Prehistoric birds couldn't have been able to fly. They had no way of getting into the air.

1. EVALUATE In which sentences is the speaker more certain?

2. EVALUATE In which sentences is the speaker less certain?

B. Discuss your answers with the class and read the Meaning and Use Notes to check them.

Meaning and Use Notes

ONLINE PRACTICE

Overview		
▶1	Modals of past possibility are used to make guesses or inferences about the past. The modal you choose shows how certain you are that something was true.	

A: Where was Jim this morning?

Less Certain	• might have, might not have, could have	B: He **might have been** outside. I'm not sure.
	• may have, may not have	C: He **may not have been** awake yet.
	• must have, must not have, have to have, have got to have	D: He **must have been** in bed. He never gets up before noon.
More Certain	• can't have, couldn't have	E: He **can't have been** upstairs. He wasn't home.

Guessing with *May Have*, *Might Have*, and *Could Have*
▶2 Use *may (not) have*, *might (not) have*, and *could have* to guess about a past situation when you don't have much proof.

Dinosaurs **may have perished** because of a climate change, or they **might have** perished because of disease. Some people think they **could have perished** because a large meteor hit Earth.

Strong Certainty with *Must Have, Have to Have*, and *Have Got to Have*

▶ **3** Use *must (not) have*, *have to have*, and *have got to have* to draw conclusions about the past when you are certain of something, and you believe there is only one logical explanation.

> **Problem:** Someone stole the money from the drawer. No one was in the room except Sally.
>
> **Conclusion:** Sally **must have taken** it.
>
> Sally **has (got) to have taken** it.

Strong Certainty with *Can't Have* and *Couldn't Have*

▶ **4A** Use *can't have* and *couldn't have* when you are certain something was unlikely or impossible.

> No one believes him. He **can't have been** home at the time of the crime. The police have evidence that he was at the crime scene.

▶ **4B** *Can't have* and *couldn't have* sometimes express surprise or disbelief about the past.

> A: You got an A on the exam.
>
> B: I **couldn't have gotten** an A! That's impossible. Didn't I get the last question wrong?

C1 Listening for Meaning and Use

▶ Notes 1–3, 4A, 4B

CD1 T47 Listen to the different opinions among archaeologists about Neanderthals. Is each speaker expressing less certainty or more certainty? Check (✓) the correct column.

	LESS CERTAINTY	MORE CERTAINTY
1.	✓	
2.		
3.		
4.		
5.		
6.		
7.		
8.		

C2 Understanding Degrees of Certainty

▶ Notes 1–3, 4A

Work with a partner. Read what two different archaeologists (A and B) have said about the "Iceman," a 5,000-year-old frozen mummy that was discovered in 1991 in the Alps. Rewrite their opinions with modals of possibility.

1. **A:** Maybe the Iceman was a shepherd.

   B: We don't believe he was a shepherd.

   A: The Iceman may have been a shepherd.
   B: He couldn't have been a shepherd.

2. **A:** It was impossible for him to build a fire.

   B: Perhaps he built a fire.

3. **A:** It is possible he froze to death.

   B: He almost certainly froze to death.

4. **A:** We can conclude that he lived in a valley.

   B: It's not likely he lived in a valley.

5. **A:** Perhaps he wasn't older than 25.

   B: We can assume he wasn't older than 25.

C3 Making Guesses and Drawing Conclusions

▶ Notes 1–3, 4A

Work in small groups. Read about a mysterious incident and discuss what might have happened. Use different affirmative and negative past modals.

Unfriendly Native Americans may have killed the first group.
The Croatoans were friendly. They can't have killed the second group.

The "Lost Colony of Roanoke" is one of the great mysteries of early American history. When John White and a group of English settlers arrived on Roanoke Island in July 1587, the only sign they found of the previous colonists were some bones. What happened is still a mystery. White quickly established good relations with the Native Americans on the nearby island of Croatoan, but a second group remained unfriendly. The settlers convinced White to sail back to England to arrange for food and supplies, but war with Spain delayed him. When he arrived three years later, in August 1590, there was no sign of the 118 settlers. Even their homes had disappeared. The only clue was the word "Croatoan" carved into a post of the fort and "Cro" carved into a tree.

Many questions remain. What happened to the first settlers? Did the second group go to live with the Croatoans? Did unfriendly natives kill them? Did they die of disease? Why was there no sign of their houses? Did they split up and go off to live in different areas?

C4 Expressing Impossibility and Disbelief

▶ Notes 4A, 4B

Work with a partner. Switch roles for each statement.

Student A: Read a statement.

Student B: Express disbelief with *couldn't have*. Give a reason for your disbelief.

1. You just won the game.

   A: You just won the game.
   B: I couldn't have won the game. I didn't even buy a ticket.

2. Your great-great-grandfather sent you a letter.

3. Your Rolls Royce ran out of gas.

4. You grew three inches taller this week.

5. You lost a million dollars yesterday.

6. You swam the English Channel last week.

C5 Writing About Impossibility and Disbelief

▶ Notes 4A, 4B

A. Do you believe everything you read in the news or on the Internet? Make a list of events or situations that you have read about that seem unbelievable. Why do you think they are unbelievable?

B. Choose one of your events or situations from part A. Write a paragraph expressing your disbelief. Tell why you think the incident couldn't have happened the way it was described. Describe what you think must have happened instead.

I found a website about the "Lost Colony of Roanoke" on the Internet yesterday. It said the colonists may have died of starvation, but I don't think this could have happened. Many historians say that the island must have had a lot of wild game, seafood, and edible plants in the late 1500s. With so much food around, the colonists couldn't have gone hungry...

D MEANING AND USE 2

Other Functions of Past Modals

 Think Critically About Meaning and Use

A. Read the sentences and answer the questions below.

a. Paul lived near his office. He could walk there every morning. He liked the exercise.

b. Paul lived near his office. He could have walked there every morning, but he broke his leg.

c. Paul lived near his office. He should have walked there every morning, but he was too lazy.

1. EVALUATE Which sentences suggest that Paul didn't walk to work every day?

2. EVALUATE Which one suggests that he did?

3. EVALUATE Which sentence expresses the speaker's opinion and advice about a past situation?

B. Discuss your answers with the class and read the Meaning and Use Notes to check them.

Meaning and Use Notes

ONLINE
PRACTICE

Past Ability and Opportunity

▶ 1   *Could have* suggests that a person had the ability or opportunity to do something in the past but <u>did not</u> do it. *Could* suggests that a person had the ability or opportunity to do something and <u>was able to</u> or <u>did</u> do it.

Could Have (Did Not Do It)

I **could have walked** to school, but I got a ride instead. (I didn't walk to school.)

You **could have spoken** French with her, but you were too shy. (You didn't speak French with her.)

Could (Did It)

I lived near the school, so I **could walk** there. (I walked to school.)

You **could speak** French at an early age. (You spoke French at an early age.)

Advice, Obligations, and Regrets About the Past

▶ **2A**   *Should(n't) have* expresses advice about past situations. *Should(n't) have* and *ought (not) to have* express past obligations (what you were or were not supposed to do). Compare the actions that the speakers actually <u>did</u> do and the actions that the speakers <u>did not</u> do.

Did Not Do It

You **should have asked** for help. (Asking for help was a good idea, but you <u>didn't</u> do it.)

She **ought to have registered** on Monday. (She was supposed to register on Monday, but she <u>didn't</u>.)

He **should have visited** his aunt in the hospital. (Visiting his aunt was the right thing to do, but he <u>didn't</u> do it.)

Did It

You **shouldn't have driven** in bad weather. (It was a bad idea to drive, but you <u>did</u> it anyway.)

He **shouldn't have taken** the money. It's illegal. (He wasn't allowed to take the money, but he <u>did</u> it anyway.)

▶ **2B**   In the first person, *should(n't) have* shows regret. It means that you think that something you did or did not do was a mistake.

Did Not Do It

I **should have accepted** the job offer. (I didn't accept the job. Now I am sorry.)

Did It

I **shouldn't have lost** my temper. (I lost my temper. It was a mistake.)

Past Permission and Necessity

▶ **3**   *May (not)* for expressing permission and *must* for expressing necessity do not have past modal forms. Several different past expressions are used instead.

Present Modals	Past Expressions		
Seniors **may have** cars.	Seniors	were permitted to / were allowed to	have cars.
Freshmen **may not have** cars.	Freshmen	were not permitted to / were not allowed to	have cars.
All visitors **must register**.	All visitors	were required to / were supposed to / had to	register.

D1 Listening for Meaning and Use

▶ Notes 1, 2A, 2B, 3

CD1 T48 Listen to the statements. Choose the sentence that best expresses the meaning of the situation that you hear.

1. **a.** John should have applied for the scholarship.

   b. John must have applied for the scholarship.

2. **a.** John could have left early.

   b. John should have left early.

3. **a.** John shouldn't have asked for help.

   b. John ought to have asked for help.

4. **a.** John must have taken two English courses.

   b. John had to take two English courses.

5. **a.** John may have registered late.

   b. John was permitted to register late.

6. **a.** John shouldn't have called his parents yesterday.

   b. John was supposed to call his parents yesterday.

7. **a.** John had to work in a department store.

   b. John could have worked in a bank.

8. **a.** I should have called John last night.

   b. I shouldn't have called John last night.

D2 Contrasting *Could* and *Could Have*

▶ Note 1

Read each situation. Choose *could* + verb or *could have* + verb.

1. When I worked downtown, I (could buy / could have bought) fresh coffee on my way to the office, so I never made any at home in the morning.

2. I (could ride / could have ridden) my bicycle to school every day, but I never did because I was afraid of the traffic.

3. We always knew when my father got off the bus because we (could see / could have seen) the bus stop from our window.

4. Why didn't anyone tell me? I (could take / could have taken) my vacation last week.

5. You (could call / could have called) me when the car broke down. Why did you leave the car on the side of the road instead?

D3 Talking About Past Opportunities ▶ Note 1

A. Work with a partner. Make up sentences about each situation using *could have* and the expressions that follow to express the different opportunities that were available to the person. Then think of one more opportunity for each situation.

Situation 1
Paul went to college. He majored in biology and education. He became a teacher, but there were other possibilities that he considered.

1. work in a lab

   He could have worked in a lab.

2. go to medical school

3. teach science in a high school

Situation 2
Lee went to cooking school. He became a chef on a cruise ship after he considered several other careers.

1. become a cook in a restaurant

2. open a restaurant

3. work in a hotel

Situation 3
Ella majored in English. She became an editor after she considered some other choices.

1. be a fiction writer

2. go to law school

3. work for a newspaper

Situation 4
Ed majored in art. He thought about other careers before he decided to paint on his own.

1. become an art teacher

2. get a job in advertising

3. do graphic design

B. On your own, think about some opportunities you had for jobs, schools, or places to live. What did you decide to do? Write four sentences describing what you could have done and a description of what you decided to do instead.

I could have lived in London, but I decided to move to New York instead.

C. Tell the class about one of your opportunities.

D4 Talking About Advice in the Past

▶ Note 2A

Work in small groups. Ask questions about each situation using *should have* and the possibilities that follow. Then give short answers with *should have* or *shouldn't have*. You can also use *could have* to express other possibilities. Explain your answers and discuss any differences in opinion you may have.

Situation 1
Ko is a foreign student who recently arrived in the United States. Last night he was invited to an American friend's house for dinner. He didn't know what to bring.

1. flowers

   A: *Should he have brought flowers?*
   B: *Yes, he should have. It's polite.* OR *He could have. Flowers are always nice.*

2. an expensive gift

3. a traditional food from his country

4. five friends with him

Situation 2
At the dinner table, he started eating before the host sat down. Then he ate his food quickly and he was still hungry.

1. wait for the host

2. eat more slowly

3. ask for more

4. wait for someone to offer him more

Situation 3
In a restaurant a few days later, Ko wanted to speak to his waiter. He didn't know how to get the waiter's attention.

1. whistle

2. snap his fingers

3. clap loudly

4. raise his hand when the waiter was looking at him

Situation 4
There was a mistake on Ko's bill at the restaurant. He didn't know what to do.

1. ignore it

2. tell the waiter

3. call the manager immediately

4. shout at the waiter

D5 Expressing Regret

▶ Note 2B

Work with a partner. Imagine that you each made these mistakes. Take turns making sentences using *should have* and *shouldn't have* to express your regret.

1. You didn't go to the movies with your friends. Everyone enjoyed the film.

   I should have gone to the movies with my friends.
   I shouldn't have stayed home last night.

2. You cooked the rice too long. It burned.

3. You left your car windows open during a rainstorm.

4. You were in a hurry at the post office. You sent an expensive birthday gift to your aunt. She never received it, and you did not insure it.

5. You didn't apply for a summer job. Now it's too late.

6. You drove over the speed limit. You got a traffic ticket.

D6 Writing About Regrets

▶ Note 2B

A. Work in small groups. Read this list of the top ten regrets that many people have. Do you agree with the list? What other regrets would you add to the list?

B. Make a list of your biggest regrets. Then write a paragraph describing a few things you think you should have done differently and tell why you feel that way. Remember to begin your paragraph with a clear topic sentence.

   My biggest regrets are all related to the fact that I moved so far away from my family. Because of the distance, I often missed holiday gatherings and last-minute lunches I could have had with my sisters. I should have stayed closer to home, and I should have visited more often. I shouldn't have...

Life's Top Ten Regrets

1	Not apologizing when you've done something wrong
2	Not traveling enough
3	Losing touch with good friends from childhood
4	Not taking time to exercise and keep fit
5	Not saving enough money for the future
6	Taking a job you knew wasn't right for you
7	Not being self-disciplined
8	Not taking your education more seriously
9	Moving away from your hometown
10	Not being more active in your town's community

Think Critically About Meaning and Use

A. Work with a partner. Read each sentence and the statements that follow. Write *T* if the statement is true or *F* if it is false.

1. I shouldn't have gone to the movies.

   _F_   **a.** I didn't go to the movies.

   _T_   **b.** I am sorry that I went to the movies.

2. He couldn't have been at work.

   _____   **a.** I don't believe that he was at work.

   _____   **b.** It's very unlikely that he was at work.

3. She ought to have called first.

   _____   **a.** She called first.

   _____   **b.** She should have called first.

4. Students may not chew gum in class.

   _____   **a.** Students are not allowed to chew gum in class.

   _____   **b.** Students were allowed to chew gum in class.

5. I should have told you.

   _____   **a.** I think I made a mistake.

   _____   **b.** I'm sorry that I didn't tell you.

6. There is only one flight from Centerville per day. They have got to be on that plane.

   _____   **a.** They can't be on the plane.

   _____   **b.** They must be on the plane.

7. I couldn't have passed my driver's test. I didn't practice at all!

   _____   **a.** I'm surprised that I passed.

   _____   **b.** I didn't pass.

8. I could go to the beach every day when I lived in Florida.

   _____   **a.** I wanted to go to the beach, but I didn't do it.

   _____   **b.** I went to the beach a lot.

Edit

Find the errors in these sentences and correct them.

1. They ~~mayn't~~ *may not* have called yet.

2. When he could have called?

3. He might a been late.

4. I ought to visited him at the hospital.

5. May he have taken the train instead of the bus?

6. She must have a cold yesterday.

7. I should have asked him. I'm sorry that I did.

8. He should have taking the exam.

9. You could of called me. I was home.

10. She have to have arrived yesterday.

11. The letter might arrived this afternoon.

12. He must had a cold yesterday.

Write

Write a review of a movie, a TV show, or a short story. Briefly summarize it and say what you liked about it. Then use past modals to discuss what you think could have or should have happened differently.

1. **BRAINSTORM** Use these categories to help you organize your ideas into three paragraphs.
   - **Summary:** What was it about? What were the important events?
   - **Strong Points:** What did you like about it?
   - **Critique:** What do you think could have or should have happened differently? What should the characters/author/producer have done differently?

2. **WRITE A FIRST DRAFT** Before you write your first draft, read the checklist below. Write your draft using past modals.

3. **EDIT** Read your work and check it against the checklist below. Circle grammar, spelling, and punctuation errors.

DO I ...	YES
organize my ideas into paragraphs?	☐
use the simple past and other past forms, as appropriate, to summarize the story and say what I liked about it?	☐
use past modals to speculate about what could have happened or been done differently?	☐

4. **PEER REVIEW** Work with a partner to help you decide how to fix your errors and improve the content. Use the checklist above.

5. **REWRITE YOUR DRAFT** Using the comments from your partner, write a final draft.

> Last night I watched a fascinating documentary on TV about the disappearance of mammoths and other megafauna in the Americas about 13,000 years ago. The show focused on four different theories about how the extinction might have occurred...

Choose the correct word or words to complete each sentence.

1. Although many linguists think there are about four or five thousand languages in the world today, others believe that there _____ many more.

   a. mustn't be
   b. maybe

   c. might be
   d. has got to

2. They _____ not be at home. All of the lights are out.

   a. must
   b. couldn't

   c. has got to
   d. don't have to

3. _____ it be snowing in New York City at the beginning of June?

   a. Could
   b. May

   c. Must
   d. Have to

4. They could _____ a lot of traffic. Maybe that's why they were so late.

   a. of had
   b. have had

   c. had had
   d. have been

5. How _____ air pollution over the past fifty years?

   a. should have controlled
   b. we should control

   c. we should have controlled
   d. should we have controlled

Choose the correct response to complete each conversation.

6. **A:** We should have registered for the yoga class.
   B: _____

   a. I'm really glad we did.
   b. It's too bad that we didn't.

   c. When did we register?
   d. You're right. We have to.

7. **A:** How much did they charge you?
   B: Last month, _____

   a. I must pay twenty-five dollars.
   b. I've got to pay twenty-five dollars.

   c. I might pay twenty-five dollars.
   d. I had to pay twenty-five dollars.

8. **A:** Did you take pictures in the museum?
   B: No, _____

   a. we must not use our cameras.
   b. we had to use our cameras.

   c. we were not allowed to use our cameras.
   d. we shouldn't have used our cameras.

Choose the correct response to complete each conversation below.

9. **A:** You may be getting a call later.

   B: _____

      a. May I?   **b.** That's good.   **c.** You won't be home.   **d.** Yes, you may.

10. **A:** I didn't sleep all night. I have a bad cough.

    B: You must be _____

       a. coughing.   **b.** sleeping.   **c.** exhausted.   **d.** at the doctor's.

11. **A:** Is the roast beef ready yet?

    B: It _____ be. It's only been in the oven for 15 minutes.

       a. ought to   **b.** mustn't   **c.** has got to   **d.** can't

Match the response to the question or statement below.

_____ **12.** Did you see that huge diamond ring?

_____ **13.** Mia lost her wallet yesterday.

_____ **14.** He hasn't returned my calls.

a. He must be exhausted.   **d.** I know. You may not like it.

b. It can't be real.   **e.** She could be on her way here.

c. She must be really upset.   **f.** He may be out of town.

Match the response to the question or statement below.

_____ **15.** You should have taken that medication.

_____ **16.** Sally arrived three hours early.

_____ **17.** When you were in high school, did you drive to school?

a. Don't worry. You'll get another one.   **e.** She must have taken the early flight.

b. No. I wasn't allowed to.   **f.** My bag was too large. I had to check it.

c. Why didn't you?   **g.** Yes, I could.

d. I'm sorry I didn't.

Complete each sentence using the past form of the modal and the verb in parentheses.

18. The mechanic _____ (ought to/check) that noise.

19. No one is answering the phone. They _____ (must/go) out.

20. _____ (I/may/leave) my ATM card at the bank. It's not in my wallet.

Appendices

1 Spelling of Verbs and Nouns Ending in -s and -es

1. For most third-person singular verbs and plural nouns, add -s to the base form.

Verbs	Nouns
swim — swims	lake — lakes

2. If the base form ends with the letters *s, z, sh, ch,* or *x*, add -es.

Verbs	Nouns
miss — misses	box — boxes

3. If the base form ends with a consonant + *y*, change *y* to *i* and add -es. (Compare vowel + *y*: obey — obeys; toy — toys.)

Verbs	Nouns
try — tries	baby — babies

4. If the base form ends with a consonant + *o*, add -s or -es. Some words take -s, -es, or both -s and -es. (Compare vowel + *o*: radio — radios; zoo — zoos.)

-s	-es	Both -s and -es
auto — autos	do — does	tornado — tornados/tornadoes
photo — photos	echo — echoes	volcano — volcanos/volcanoes
piano — pianos	go — goes	zero — zeros/zeroes
solo — solos	hero — heroes	
	potato — potatoes	
	tomato — tomatoes	

5. If the base form of certain nouns ends in a single *f* or in *fe*, change the *f* or *fe* to *v* and add -es.

   calf — calves
   shelf — shelves
   knife — knives

   Exceptions

   belief — beliefs
   chief — chiefs
   roof — roofs
   scarf — scarfs/scarves

2 Pronunciation of Verbs and Nouns Ending in -s and -es

1. If the base form of the verb or noun ends with the sounds /s/, /z/, /ʃ/, /ʒ/, /tʃ/, /dʒ/, or /ks/, then pronounce -es as an extra syllable /ɪz/.

Verbs		Nouns	
slice — slices	watch — watches	price — prices	inch — inches
lose — loses	judge — judges	size — sizes	language — languages
wash — washes	relax — relaxes	dish — dishes	tax — taxes
		garage — garages	

2. If the base form ends with the voiceless sounds /p/, /t/, /k/, /f/, or /θ/, then pronounce -s and -es as /s/.

Verbs		Nouns	
sleep — sleeps	work — works	grape — grapes	cuff — cuffs
hit — hits	laugh — laughs	cat — cats	fifth — fifths
		book — books	

3. If the base form ends with any other consonant or with a vowel sound, then pronounce -s and -es as /z/.

Verbs	Nouns
learn — learns	name — names
go — goes	boy — boys

3 Spelling of Verbs Ending in -ing

1. For most verbs, add -ing to the base form of the verb.

sleep — sleeping   talk — talking

2. If the base form ends in a single e, drop the e and add -ing (exception: be – being).

live — living   write — writing

3. If the base form ends in ie, change ie to y and add -ing.

die — dying   lie — lying

4. If the base form of a one-syllable verb ends with a single vowel + consonant, double the final consonant and add -ing. (Compare two vowels + consonant: eat — eating.)

hit — hitting   stop — stopping

5. If the base form of a verb with two or more syllables ends in a single vowel + consonant, double the final consonant only if the stress is on the final syllable. Do not double the final consonant if the stress is not on the final syllable.

admit — admitting   begin — beginning   develop — developing   listen — listening

6. Do not double the final consonants x, w, and y.

fix — fixing   plow — plowing   obey — obeying

4   Spelling of Verbs Ending in -ed

1. To form the simple past and past participle of most regular verbs, add *-ed* to the base form.

   brush — brushed   play — played

2. If the base form ends with *e*, just add *-d*.

   close — closed   live — lived

3. If the base form ends with a consonant + *y*, change the *y* to *i* and add *-ed*. (Compare vowel +*y*: play — played; enjoy — enjoyed.)

   study — studied   dry — dried

4. If the base form of a one-syllable verb ends with a single vowel + consonant, double the final consonant and add *-ed*.

   plan — planned   shop — shopped

5. If the base form of a verb with two or more syllables ends in a single vowel + consonant, double the final consonant and add *-ed* only when the stress is on the final syllable. Do not double the final consonant if the stress is not on the final syllable.

   prefér — preferred   énter — entered

6. Do not double the final consonants *x*, *w*, and *y*.

   coax — coaxed   snow — snowed   stay — stayed

5   Pronunciation of Verbs Ending in -ed

1. If the base form of the verb ends with the sounds /t/ or /d/, then pronounce *-ed* as an extra syllable /ɪd/.

/t/	/d/
start — started	need — needed
wait — waited	decide — decided

2. If the base form ends with the voiceless sounds /f/, /k/, /p/, /s/, /ʃ/, /tʃ/, or /ks/, then pronounce *-ed* as /t/.

laugh — laughed	jump — jumped	wish — wished	fax — faxed
look — looked	slice — sliced	watch — watched	

3. If the base form ends with the voiced sounds /b/, /g/, /dʒ/, /m/, /n/, /ŋ/, /l/, /r/, /ð/, /v/, /z/, or with a vowel, then pronounce *-ed* as /d/.

rob — robbed	hum — hummed	call — called	wave — waved
brag — bragged	rain — rained	order — ordered	close — closed
judge — judged	bang — banged	bathe — bathed	play — played

6 Irregular Verbs

Base Form	Simple Past	Past Participle	Base Form	Simple Past	Past Participle
arise	arose	arisen	forget	forgot	forgotten
be	was/were	been	forgive	forgave	forgiven
beat	beat	beaten	freeze	froze	frozen
become	became	become	get	got	gotten
begin	began	begun	give	gave	given
bend	bent	bent	go	went	gone
bet	bet	bet	grind	ground	ground
bind	bound	bound	grow	grew	grown
bite	bit	bitten	hang	hung	hung
bleed	bled	bled	have	had	had
blow	blew	blown	hear	heard	heard
break	broke	broken	hide	hid	hidden
bring	brought	brought	hit	hit	hit
build	built	built	hold	held	held
burst	burst	burst	hurt	hurt	hurt
buy	bought	bought	keep	kept	kept
catch	caught	caught	know	knew	known
choose	chose	chosen	lay (= put)	laid	laid
cling	clung	clung	lead	led	led
come	came	come	leave	left	left
cost	cost	cost	lend	lent	lent
creep	crept	crept	let	let	let
cut	cut	cut	lie (= recline)	lay	lain
deal	dealt	dealt	light	lit	lit
dig	dug	dug	lose	lost	lost
dive	dove/dived	dived	make	made	made
do	did	done	mean	meant	meant
draw	drew	drawn	meet	met	met
drink	drank	drunk	pay	paid	paid
drive	drove	driven	prove	proved	proven/proved
eat	ate	eaten	put	put	put
fall	fell	fallen	quit	quit	quit
feed	fed	fed	read	read	read
feel	felt	felt	ride	rode	ridden
fight	fought	fought	ring	rang	rung
find	found	found	rise	rose	risen
fit	fit	fit	run	ran	run
flee	fled	fled	say	said	said
fly	flew	flown	see	saw	seen
forbid	forbade	forbidden	seek	sought	sought

Base Form	Simple Past	Past Participle	Base Form	Simple Past	Past Participle
sell	sold	sold	sting	stung	stung
send	sent	sent	stink	stank	stunk
set	set	set	strike	struck	struck
sew	sewed	sewn	string	strung	strung
shake	shook	shaken	swear	swore	sworn
shine	shone	shone	sweep	swept	swept
shoot	shot	shot	swim	swam	swum
show	showed	shown	swing	swung	swung
shrink	shrank	shrunk	take	took	taken
shut	shut	shut	teach	taught	taught
sing	sang	sung	tear	tore	torn
sink	sank	sunk	tell	told	told
sit	sat	sat	think	thought	thought
sleep	slept	slept	throw	threw	thrown
slide	slid	slid	understand	understood	understood
speak	spoke	spoken	undertake	undertook	undertaken
speed	sped	sped	upset	upset	upset
spend	spent	spent	wake	woke	woken
spin	spun	spun	wear	wore	worn
split	split	split	weave	wove	woven
spread	spread	spread	weep	wept	wept
spring	sprang	sprung	wet	wet	wet
stand	stood	stood	win	won	won
steal	stole	stolen	wind	wound	wound
stick	stuck	stuck	write	wrote	written

7 Common Intransitive Verbs

These verbs can only be used intransitively. (They cannot be followed by an object.)

ache	emerge	itch	sit
appear	erupt	laugh	sleep
arrive	faint	live	smile
be	fall	look	snow
come	frown	matter	stand
cry	go	occur	stay
depart	grin	rain	talk
die	happen	remain	weep
disappear	hesitate	seem	

8 Gerunds

Verb + Gerund

These verbs may be followed by gerunds, but not by infinitives:

acknowledge	detest	keep (= continue)	recall
admit	discuss	loathe	recollect
anticipate	dislike	mean (= involve)	recommend
appreciate	endure	mention	regret
avoid	enjoy	mind (= object to)	report
can't help	escape	miss	resent
celebrate	excuse	omit	resist
consider	feel like	postpone	resume
defend	finish	practice	risk
defer	go	prevent	suggest
delay	imagine	prohibit	tolerate
deny	involve	quit	understand

Verb with Preposition + Gerund

These verbs or verb phrases with prepositions may be followed by gerunds, but not by infinitives:

adapt to	believe in	depend on
adjust to	blame for	disapprove of
agree (with someone) on	care about	discourage (someone) from
apologize (to someone) for	complain (to someone) about	engage in
approve of	concentrate on	forgive (someone) for
argue (with someone) about	consist of	help (someone) with
ask about	decide on	

Be + Adjective + Preposition + Gerund

Adjectives with prepositions typically occur in be + adjective phrases. These phrases may be followed by gerunds, but not by infinitives:

be accustomed to	be famous for	be proud of
be afraid of	be fond of	be responsible for
be angry (at someone) about	be glad about	be sad about
be ashamed of	be good at	be successful in
be capable of	be happy about	be suitable for
be certain of/about	be incapable of	be tired of
be concerned with	be interested in	be tolerant of
be critical of	be jealous of	be upset about
be discouraged from	be known for	be used to
be enthusiastic about	be nervous about	be useful for
be familiar with	be perfect for	be worried about

9 Infinitives

These verbs may be followed by infinitives, but not by gerunds:

Verb + Infinitive

agree	decide	manage	struggle
aim	decline	plan	swear
appear	demand	pledge	tend
arrange	fail	pretend	volunteer
care	guarantee	refuse	wait
claim	hope	resolve	
consent	intend	seem	

Verb + Object + Infinitive

advise	get	persuade	tell
command	hire	remind	trust
convince	invite	require	urge
force	order	teach	warn

Verb + (Object) + Infinitive

ask	desire	need	promise
beg	expect	offer	want
choose	help	pay	wish
dare	know	prepare	would like

Adjective + Infinitive

afraid	distressed	hesitant	reluctant
alarmed	disturbed	impossible	right
amazed	eager	interested	sad
anxious	easy	likely	scared
astonished	embarrassed	lucky	shocked
careful	excited	necessary	sorry
curious	fascinated	pleased	surprised
delighted	fortunate	possible	unlikely
depressed	frightened	prepared	unnecessary
determined	glad	proud	willing
difficult	happy	ready	wrong
disappointed	hard	relieved	

10 Verb + Infinitive or Gerund

These verbs may be followed by infinitives or gerunds:

attempt	cease	like	propose	stop
begin	continue	love	regret	try
can't bear	forget	neglect	remember	
can't stand	hate	prefer	start	

11 Mental Activity Verbs

These mental activity verbs are followed by noun clauses:

agree	decide	find (out)	learn	recognize
assume	discover	forget	mean	regret
believe	doubt	guess	notice	remember
bet	dream	hear	pretend	suppose
calculate	expect	hope	prove	think
conclude	feel	imagine	realize	understand
consider	figure out	know	recall	wonder

12 Reporting Verbs

Verb + Noun Clause

These reporting verbs are followed by noun clauses:

acknowledge	conclude	instruct (someone)	report
add	confess	maintain	respond
admit	confirm	mention	roar
advise (someone)	convince (someone)	murmur	say
affirm	cry	mutter	scream
agree	declare	note	shout
announce	demand	notify (someone)	shriek
answer	deny	observe	sneer
argue	emphasize	persuade (someone)	stammer
ask	estimate	point out	state
assert	exclaim	promise	suggest
assure (someone)	explain	propose	swear
boast	grumble	protest	tell (someone)
brag	guess	recommend	threaten
caution	imply	remark	
claim	indicate	remind (someone)	
comment	inform (someone)	repeat	
complain	insist	reply	

Verb + Infinitive

These reporting verbs are used with infinitives:

advise (someone) to
ask (someone) to
beg (someone) to
command (someone) to
direct (someone) to

forbid (someone) to
instruct (someone) to
oblige (someone) to
order (someone) to
request (someone) to

tell (someone) to
urge (someone) to
want (someone) to

13 Punctuation Rules for Quoted Speech

1. If quoted speech comes after the reporting verb:

   - Place a comma after the reporting verb.
   - Place quotation marks at the beginning and end of reported speech. Put them near the top of the letter.
   - Begin quoted speech with a capital letter.
   - Use the correct punctuation (a period, an exclamation mark, or a question mark) and place the punctuation inside the quotation marks.

   Examples
   He said, "We are staying."
   He shouted, "We are staying!"
   He asked me, "Are we staying?"

2. If quoted speech comes before the reporting verb:

   - Place quotation marks at the beginning and end of reported speech. Put them near the top of the letter.
   - Begin quoted speech with a capital letter.
   - Use a comma if the quoted speech is a statement. Use an exclamation if the quoted speech is an exclamation. Use a question mark if the quoted speech is a question. Place the punctuation inside the quotation marks.
   - Begin the phrase that follows the quoted speech with a lowercase letter.
   - Use a period at the end of the main sentence.

   Examples
   "We are staying," he said.
   "We are staying!" he shouted.
   "Are we staying?" he asked me.

14 Contractions with Verb and Modal Forms

Contractions with *Be*

I am	= I'm
you are	= you're
he is	= he's
she is	= she's
it is	= it's
we are	= we're
you are	= you're
they are	= they're

I am not	= I'm not
you are not	= you're not / you aren't
he is not	= he's not / he isn't
she is not	= she's not / she isn't
it is not	= it's not / it isn't
we are not	= we're not / we aren't
you are not	= you're not / you aren't
they are not	= they're not / they aren't

Contractions with *Be Going To*

I am going to	= I'm going to
you are going to	= you're going to
he is going to	= he's going to
she is going to	= she's going to
it is going to	= it's going to
we are going to	= we're going to
you are going to	= you're going to
they are going to	= they're going to
you are not going to	= you're not going to / you aren't going to

Contractions with *Will*

I will	= I'll
you will	= you'll
he will	= he'll
she will	= she'll
it will	= it'll
we will	= we'll
you will	= you'll
they will	= they'll
will not	= won't

Contractions with *Would*

I would	= I'd
you would	= you'd
he would	= he'd
she would	= she'd
we would	= we'd
you would	= you'd
they would	= they'd
would not	= wouldn't

Contractions with *Was* and *Were*

was not	= wasn't
were not	= weren't

Contractions with *Have*

I have	= I've
you have	= you've
he has	= he's
she has	= she's
it has	= it's
we have	= we've
you have	= you've
they have	= they've
have not	= haven't
has not	= hasn't

Contractions with *Had*

I had	= I'd
you had	= you'd
he had	= he'd
she had	= she'd
it had	= it'd
we had	= we'd
you had	= you'd
they had	= they'd
had not	= hadn't

Contractions with *Do* and *Did*

do not	= don't
does not	= doesn't
did not	= didn't

Contractions with Modals and Phrasal Modals

cannot/can not	= can't
could not	= couldn't
should not	= shouldn't
have got to	= 've got to
has got to	= 's got to

15 Phrasal Verbs

Separable Phrasal Verbs

Many two-word phrasal verbs are separable. This means that a noun object can separate the two words of the phrasal verb or follow the phrasal verb. If the object is a pronoun (*me, you, him, her, it, us, them*), the pronoun must separate the two words.

Noun Object	Pronoun Object
She **turned** the offer **down**.	She **turned** it **down**.
She **turned down** the offer.	x She turned down it. (INCORRECT)

These are some common separable phrasal verbs and their meanings:

Phrasal Verb	Meaning
ask (someone) out	invite someone to go out
ask (someone) over	invite someone to come to your house
blow (something) up	inflate, cause something to explode
boot (something) up	start or get a computer ready for use
bring (someone) up	raise a child
bring (something) up	introduce or call attention to a topic
burn (something) down	destroy by fire
call (someone) back	return a phone call to someone
call (something) off	cancel something
call (someone) up	telephone
call (something) up	retrieve from the memory of a computer
check (something) out	borrow a book, tape, video from the library; verify
clean (something) out	clean the inside of something thoroughly
clean (something) up	clean thoroughly and remove anything unwanted
clear (something) up	explain a problem
cross (something) out	draw a line through
cut (something) up	cut into little pieces
do (something) over	do something again
figure (something) out	solve a problem
fill (something) in	write in a blank or a space
fill (something) out	write information on a form
fill (something) up	fill completely with something
find (something) out	discover information
give (something) back	return something
give (something) up	quit something; get rid of something
hand (something) in	submit homework, a test, an application
hand (something) out	distribute something
hang (something) up	put on a clothes hanger; end a telephone call
keep (someone) up	prevent someone from going to sleep
kick (someone) out	force someone to leave
leave (something) out	omit

Phrasal Verb	Meaning
look (something) over	examine carefully
look (something) up	look for information in a book
make (something) up	create or invent something; do work that was missed
make (something) up to (someone)	return a favor to someone
pay (someone) back	return money owned to someone
pick (something) out	choose
pick (something/someone) up	lift something or someone; stop to get something or someone
point (something) out	mention, draw attention to something
put (something) away	put something in its usual place
put (something) back	return something to its original place
put (something) down	stop holding something
put (something) in	install
put (something) off	postpone
put (something) on	get dressed
put (something) out	extinguish a fire, cigarette, or cigar
put (something) over on (someone)	deceive someone
set (something) up	make something ready for use
shut (something) off	turn off a machine
start (something) over	start again
take (something) away	remove
take (a time period) off	have a break from work or school
take (something) off	remove
take (someone) out	accompany to the theater, a restaurant, a movie
take (something) out	remove something from something else
tear (something) down	destroy completely
tear (something) off	detach something
tear (something) up	tear into pieces
think (something) over	reflect upon something before making a decision
think (something) up	invent
throw (something) away	put something in the trash
throw (something) out	put something in the trash
try (something) on	put on clothing to see how it looks
turn (something) down	lower the volume; refuse an offer or invitation
turn (something) in	return; submit homework, a test, an application
turn (something) off	stop a machine or light
turn (something) on	start a machine or light
turn (something) up	increase the volume
use (something) up	use something until no more is left
wake (someone) up	cause someone to stop sleeping
wear (someone) out	cause someone to become exhausted
work (something) out	solve something
write (something) down	write something on a piece of paper

Nonseparable Phrasal Verbs

Some two-word verbs and most three-word verbs are nonseparable. This means that a noun or pronoun object cannot separate the two parts of the phrasal verb.

Noun Object

The teacher **went over** the lesson.

x The teacher went the lesson over. (INCORRECT)

Pronoun Object

The teacher **went over** it.

x The teacher went it over. (INCORRECT)

These are some common nonseparable phrasal verbs and their meanings:

Phrasal Verb	Meaning
blow up	explode
break down	stop functioning properly
break up with (someone)	end a relationship with someone
burn down	be destroyed by fire
call on (someone)	ask someone to answer or speak in class
catch up with (someone/something)	travel fast enough to overtake someone who is ahead
check out of (a hotel)	leave a hotel after paying the bill
clear up	become fair weather
come back	return
come over	visit
come up with (something)	think of a plan or reply
cut down on (something)	reduce
eat out	have a meal in a restaurant
face up to (something)	be brave enough to accept or deal with
fall down	leave a standing position; perform in a disappointing way
get away with (doing something)	not be punished for doing something wrong
get down to (something)	begin to give serious attention to
get off (something)	leave a plane, bus, train
get on (something)	enter a plane, bus, train
get over (something)	recover from an illness or serious life event
get up	arise from a bed or chair
give up	stop trying, lose hope
go back	return
go down	(of computers) stop functioning; (of prices or temperature) become lower; (of ships) sink; (of the sun or moon) set
go off	stop functioning; (of alarms) start functioning; explode or make a loud noise
go on	take place, happen
go out	leave one's house to go to a social event
go out with (someone)	spend time regularly with someone
go over (something)	review
grow up	become an adult

Phrasal Verb	Meaning
hold on	wait on the telephone
keep on (doing something)	continue doing something
keep up with	stay at the same level or position
look out for (something/someone)	be careful of something or someone
move out	stop occupying a residence, especially by removing one's possessions
pack up	prepare all of one's belongings for moving
put up with (something/someone)	tolerate
run out	come to an end, be completely used up
run out of (something)	have no more of something
show up	appear, be seen, arrive at a place
sit down	get into a seated position
stay out	remain out of the house, especially at night
stay up	remain awake, not go to bed
take off	leave (usually by plane)
turn up	appear
wake up	stop sleeping
work out	exercise vigorously

16 Phonetic Symbols

Vowels

i	see /si/	u	too /tu/	oʊ	go /goʊ/
ɪ	sit /sɪt/	ʌ	cup /kʌp/	ər	bird /bərd/
ɛ	ten /tɛn/	ə	about /əˈbaʊt/	ɪr	near /nɪr/
æ	cat /kæt/	eɪ	say /seɪ/	ɛr	hair /hɛr/
ɑ	hot /hɑt/	aɪ	five /faɪv/	ɑr	car /kɑr/
ɔ	saw /sɔ/	ɔɪ	boy /bɔɪ/	ɔr	north /nɔrθ/
ʊ	put /pʊt/	aʊ	now /naʊ/	ʊr	tour /tʊr/

Consonants

p	pen /pɛn/	f	fall /fɔl/	m	man /mæn/
b	bad /bæd/	v	voice /vɔɪs/	n	no /noʊ/
t	tea /ti/	θ	thin /θɪn/	ŋ	sing /sɪŋ/
t̮	butter /ˈbʌt̮ər/	ð	then /ðɛn/	l	leg /lɛg/
d	did /dɪd/	s	so /soʊ/	r	red /rɛd/
k	cat /kæt/	z	zoo /zu/	j	yes /jɛs/
g	got /gɑt/	ʃ	she /ʃi/	w	wet /wɛt/
tʃ	chin /tʃɪn/	ʒ	vision /ˈvɪʒn/		
dʒ	June /dʒun/	h	how /haʊ/		

Glossary of Grammar Terms

ability modal *See* **modal of ability**.

active sentence In active sentences, the agent (the noun that is performing the action) is in subject position and the receiver (the noun that receives or is a result of the action) is in object position. In the following sentence, the subject **Alex** performed the action, and the object **letter** received the action.

> Alex mailed the letter.

adjective A word that describes or modifies the meaning of a noun.

> the **orange** car   a **strange** noise

adjective clause *See* **relative clause**.

adjective phrase A phrase that functions as an adjective.

> These shoes are **too tight**.

adverb A word that describes or modifies the meaning of a verb, another adverb, an adjective, or a sentence. Adverbs answer such questions as *How? When? Where?* or *How often?* They often end in **-ly**.

> She ran **quickly**.   She ran **very** quickly.
> a **really** hot day   **Maybe** she'll leave.

adverb of frequency An adverb that tells how often a situation occurs. Adverbs of frequency range in meaning from *all of the time* to *none of the time*.

> She **always** eats breakfast.
> He **never** eats meat.

adverbial phrase A phrase that functions as an adverb.

> Amy spoke **very softly**.

affirmative statement A positive sentence that does not have a negative verb.

> Linda went to the movies.

agent The noun that is performing the action in a sentence. *See* **active sentence, passive sentence.**

> The letter was mailed by **Alex**.

agentless passive A passive sentence that doesn't mention an agent.

> The letter was mailed.

agreement The subject and verb of a clause must agree in number. If the subject is singular, the verb form is also singular. If the subject is plural, the verb form is also plural.

> **He comes** home early.
> **They come** home early.

article The words **a, an**, and **the** in English. Articles are used to introduce and identify nouns.

> **a** potato   **an** onion   **the** supermarket

auxiliary verb A verb that is used before main verbs (or other auxiliary verbs) in a sentence. Auxiliary verbs are usually used in questions and negative sentences. **Do**, **have**, and **be** can act as auxiliary verbs. Modals (**may**, **can**, **will**, and so on) are also auxiliary verbs.

> **Do** you have the time?
> I **have** never been to Italy.
> The suitcase **was** taken.   I **may** be late.

base form The form of a verb without any verb endings; the infinitive form without *to*. Also called *simple form*.

> sleep   be   stop

clause A group of words that has a subject and a verb. *See also* **dependent clause** and **main clause**.

> If I leave,...   The rain stopped.
> ...when he speaks.   ...that I saw.

common noun A noun that refers to any of a class of people, animals, places, things, or ideas. Common nouns are not capitalized.

> man   cat   city   pencil   grammar

communication verb *See* **reporting verb**.

comparative A form of an adjective, adverb, or noun that is used to express differences between two items or situations.

This book is **heavier than** that one.
He runs **more quickly than** his brother.
A CD costs **more money than** a cassette.

complex sentence A sentence that has a main clause and one or more dependent clauses.

When the bell rang, we were finishing dinner.

conditional sentence A sentence that expresses a real or unreal situation in the *if* clause, and the (real or unreal) expected result in the main clause.

If I have time, I will travel to Africa.
If I had time, I would travel to Africa.

contraction The combination of two words into one by omitting certain letters and replacing them with an apostrophe.

I will = **I'll**   we are = **we're**   are not = **aren't**

count noun A common noun that can be counted. It usually has both a singular and a plural form.

orange — oranges   woman — women

defining relative clause *See* **restrictive relative clause**.

definite article The word **the** in English. It is used to identify nouns based on assumptions about what information the speaker and listener share about the noun. The definite article is also used for making general statements about a whole class or group of nouns.

Please give me **the** key.
The scorpion is dangerous.

dependent clause A clause that cannot stand alone as a sentence because it depends on the main clause to complete the meaning of the sentence. Also called *subordinate clause*.

I'm going home **after he calls**.

determiner A word such as **a, an, the, this, that, these, those, my, some, a few,** and **three,** that is used before a noun to limit its meaning in some way.

those videos

direct speech *See* **quoted speech**.

embedded question *See* **wh- clause**.

future A time that is to come. The future is expressed in English with **will**, **be going to**, the simple present, or the present continuous. These different forms of the future often have different meanings and uses. *See also* **future continuous**.

I **will** help you later.
David **is going to** call later.
The train **leaves** at 6:05 this evening.
I'm driving to Toronto tomorrow.

future continuous A verb form that expresses an activity in progress at a specific time in the future. It is formed with **will** + **be** + main verb + **-ing**.

I'll be leaving for Hawaii at noon tomorrow.

general quantity expression A quantity expression that indicates whether a quantity or an amount is large or small. It does not give an exact amount.

a lot of cookies   **a little** flour

general statement A generalization about a whole class or group of nouns.

Whales are mammals.
A daffodil is a flower that grows from a bulb.

generic noun A noun that refers to a whole class or group of nouns.

I like **rice**.
A bird can fly.
The laser is an important tool.

gerund An **-ing** form of a verb that is used in place of a noun or pronoun to name an activity or a situation.

Skiing is fun.   He doesn't like **being sick**.

identifying relative clause *See* **restrictive relative clause**.

***if* clause** A dependent clause that begins with **if** and expresses a real or unreal situation.

If I have the time, I'll paint the kitchen.
If I had the time, I'd paint the kitchen.

***if/whether* clause** A noun clause that begins with either **if** or **whether**.

I don't know **if they're here**.
I don't know **whether or not they're here**.

imperative A type of sentence, usually without a subject, that tells someone to do something. The verb is in the base form.

Open your books to page 36.
Be ready at eight.

impersonal *you* The use of the pronoun **you** to refer to people in general rather than a particular person or group of people.

Nowadays, **you** can buy anything on the Internet.

indefinite article The words **a** and **an** in English. Indefinite articles introduce a noun as a member of a class of nouns, or make generalizations about a whole class or group of nouns.

Please hand me **a** pencil.
An ocean is **a** large body of water.

independent clause *See* **main clause**.

indirect question *See* **wh- clause**.

indirect speech *See* **reported speech**.

infinitive A verb form that includes **to** + the base form of a verb. An infinitive is used in place of a noun or pronoun to name an activity or situation expressed by a verb.

Do you like **to swim**?

information question A question that begins with a **wh-** word.

Where does she live? Who lives here?

intransitive verb A verb that cannot be followed by an object.

We finally **arrived**.

irregular verb A verb that forms the simple past in a different way than regular verbs.

put — put — put   buy — bought — bought

main clause A clause that can be used by itself as a sentence. Also called *independent clause*.

I'm going home.

main verb A verb that can be used alone in a sentence. A main verb can also occur with an auxiliary verb.

I **ate** lunch at 11:30.
Kate can't **eat** lunch today.

mental activity verb A verb such as **decide, know**, and **understand**, that expresses an opinion, thought, or feeling.

I don't **know** why she left.

modal The auxiliary verbs **can, could, may, might, must, should, will**, and **would**. They modify the meaning of a main verb by expressing ability, authority, formality, politeness, or various degrees of certainty. Also called *modal auxiliary*.

You **should** take something for your headache.
Applicants **must** have a high school diploma.

modal of ability **Can** and **could** are called modals of ability when they express knowledge, skill, opportunity, and capability.

He **can** speak Arabic and English.
Can you play the piano?
Yesterday we **couldn't** leave during the storm.
Seat belts **can** save lives.

modal of possibility **Could, might, may, should, must**, and **will** are called modals of possibility when they express various degrees of certainty ranging from slight possibility to strong certainty.

It **could / might / may / will** rain later.

modal auxiliary *See* **modal**.

modify To add to or change the meaning of a word.

expensive cars (The adjective **expensive** modifies **cars**.)

noncount noun A common noun that cannot be counted. A noncount noun has no plural form and cannot occur with **a, an**, or a number.

information   mathematics   weather

nondefining relative clause *See* **nonrestrictive relative clause**.

nonidentifying relative clause *See* **nonrestrictive relative clause**.

nonrestrictive relative clause A relative clause that adds extra information about the noun that it modifies. This information is not necessary to identify the noun, and it can be omitted. Also called *nondefining* or *nonidentifying relative clause*.

Rick, **who is seven**, plays hockey.

nonseparable Refers to two- or three-word verbs that don't allow a noun or pronoun object to separate the two or three words in the verb phrase. Certain two-word verbs and almost all three-word verbs are nonseparable.

> Amy **got off** the bus.
> We **cut down on** fat in our diet.

noun A word that typically refers to a person, animal, place, thing, or idea.

> Tom rabbit store computer mathematics

noun clause A dependent clause that can occur in the same place as a noun, pronoun, or noun phrase in a sentence. Noun clauses begin with **wh-** words, **if**, **whether**, or **that**.

> I don't know **where he is**.
> I wonder **if he's coming**.
> I don't know **whether it's true**.
> I think **that it's a lie**.

noun phrase A phrase formed by a noun and its modifiers. A noun phrase can substitute for a noun in a sentence.

> She drank **milk**.
> She drank **chocolate milk**.
> She drank **the milk**.

object A noun, pronoun, or noun phrase that follows a transitive verb or a preposition.

> Steve threw **the ball**.
> She likes **him**.
> Go with **her**.

object relative pronoun A relative pronoun that is the object of a relative clause. It comes before the subject noun or pronoun of the relative clause.

> the letter **that / which** I wrote
> the man **who / whom** I saw

passive sentence Passive sentences emphasize the receiver of an action by changing the usual order of the subject and object in a sentence. The subject (**The letter**) does not perform the action; it receives the action or is the result of an action. The passive is formed with a form of **be** + the past participle of a transitive verb.

> The letter was mailed yesterday.

past continuous A verb form that expresses an action or situation in progress at a specific time in the past. The past continuous is formed with **was** or **were** + verb + **-ing**. Also called *past progressive*.

> A: What **were** you **doing** last night at eight o'clock?
> B: I **was studying**.

past modal A modal that is used to express past certainty, past obligations, and past abilities or opportunities. It is formed with a modal + **have** + past participle of the main verb. Also called *perfect modal*.

> He **must have arrived** late.
> I **should have called**, but I forgot.
> We **could have come**, but no one told us.

past participle A past verb form that may differ from the simple past form of some irregular verbs. It is used to form the present perfect, present perfect continuous, past perfect, past perfect continuous, and the passive.

> I have never **seen** that movie.
> He's **been** working too much lately.
> By noon, we had already **taken** the exam.
> She had **been** working since 8:30.
> The letter was **sent** on Monday.

past perfect A verb form that expresses a relationship between two past times. The past perfect indicates the earlier event or situation. It is formed with **had** + the past participle of the main verb.

> I **had** already **left** when she called.

past perfect continuous A verb form that is like the past perfect, but it emphasizes the duration of the earlier event or situation. It is formed with **had** + **been** + main verb + **-ing**.

> When I was offered the position, I **had been looking** for a new job for several months.

past perfect progressive *See* **past perfect continuous**.

past progressive *See* **past continuous**.

past phrasal modal Examples of past phrasal modals are **ought to have**, **have to have**, and **have got to have**.

past unreal conditional sentence A **conditional** sentence that expresses an unreal condition about the past and its imaginary result. It has an **if** clause in the past perfect and a main clause with **would have** + the past participle of the main verb.

> If I had been smarter, I would have complained to the manager.

past *wish* sentence A **wish** sentence that expresses a desire for something that didn't actually happen in the past. It is formed with a **wish** clause + a past perfect clause.

> I wish I had moved to Colorado.

perfect modal *See* **past modal.**

phrasal modal A verb that is not a true modal, but has the same meaning as a modal verb. Examples of phrasal modals are **ought to, have to,** and **have got to.**

phrasal verb A two- or three-word verb such as **turn down** or **run out of**. The meaning of a phrasal verb is usually different from the meanings of its individual words.

> She **turned down** the job offer.
> Don't **run out of** gas on the freeway.

phrase A group of words that can form a grammatical unit. A phrase can take the form of a noun phrase, verb phrase, adjective phrase, adverbial phrase, or prepositional phrase. This means it can act as a noun, verb, adjective, adverb, or preposition.

> The **tall man** left.
> Lee **hit the ball.**
> The child was **very quiet.**
> She spoke **too fast.**
> They ran **down the stairs.**

possibility modal *See* **modal of possibility.**

preposition A word such as **at, in, on,** or **to,** that links nouns, pronouns, and gerunds to other words.

prepositional phrase A phrase that consists of a preposition followed by a noun or noun phrase.

> on Sunday   under the table

present continuous A verb form that indicates that an action is in progress, temporary, or changing. It is formed with **be** + verb + **-ing**. Also called *present progressive.*

> I'm **watering** the garden.
> Ruth **is working** for her uncle.
> He's **getting** better.

present perfect A verb form that expresses a connection between the past and the present. It indicates indefinite past time, recent past time, or continuing past time. The present perfect is formed with **have** + the past participle of the main verb.

> I've **seen** that movie.
> The manager **has** just **resigned.**
> We've **been** here for three hours.

present perfect continuous A verb form that focuses on the duration of actions that began in the past and continue into the present or have just ended. It is formed with **have** + **been** + verb + **-ing**.

> They've **been waiting** for an hour.
> I've **been watering** the garden.

present perfect progressive *See* **present perfect continuous.**

present progressive *See* **present continuous.**

pronoun A word that can replace a noun or noun phrase. **I, you, he, she, it, mine,** and **yours** are some examples of pronouns.

proper noun A noun that is the name of a particular person, animal, place, thing, or idea. Proper nouns begin with capital letters and are usually not preceded by *the.*

> Peter   Rover   India   Apollo 13   Buddhism

purpose infinitive An infinitive that expresses the reason or purpose for doing something.

> **In order to operate this machine,** press the green button.

quantity expression A word or words that occur before a noun to express a quantity or amount of that noun.

> **a lot of** rain   **few** books   **four** trucks

quoted speech The form of a sentence that uses the exact words of a speaker or writer. Written quoted speech uses quotation marks. Also called *direct speech*.

"**Where did you go?**" he asked.

real conditional sentence A sentence that expresses a real or possible situation in the **if** clause and the expected result in the main clause. It has an **if** clause in the simple present, and the **will** future in the main clause.

If I get a raise, I won't look for a new job.

receiver The noun that receives or is the result of an action in a sentence. See **active sentence**, **passive sentence**.

The letter was mailed by Alex.

regular verb A verb that forms the simple past by adding -**ed**, -**d**, or changing **y** to **i** and then adding -**ed** to the simple form.

hunt — hunted   love — loved   cry — cried

rejoinder A short response used in conversation.

A: I like sushi.
B: **Me too**.
C: **So do I**.

relative clause A clause that modifies a preceding noun. Relative clauses generally begin with **who**, **whom**, **that**, **which**, and **whose**.

The man **who called** is my cousin.
We saw the elephant **that was just born**.

relative pronoun A pronoun that begins a relative clause and refers to a noun in the main clause. The words **who**, **whom**, **that**, **which**, and **whose** are relative pronouns.

reported speech A form of a sentence that expresses the meaning of quoted speech or writing from the point of view of the reporter. **Wh**- clauses, **if/whether** clauses, and **that** clauses are used to express reported speech after a reporting verb.

He explained why he was late.
He said that he was tired.
We asked if they could come early.

reporting verb A verb such as **say**, **tell**, **ask**, **explain**, and **complain** that is used to express what has been said or written in both quoted speech and reported speech.

Tony **complained**, "I'm tired."
Tony **complained** that he was tired.

restrictive relative clause A relative clause that gives information that helps identify or define the noun that it modifies. In the following sentence, the speaker has more than one aunt. The relative clause **who speaks Russian** identifies which aunt the speaker is talking about. Also called *defining* or *identifying relative clause*.

My aunt **who speaks Russian** is an interpreter.

separable Refers to certain two-word verbs that allow a noun or pronoun object to separate the two words in the verb phrase.

She **gave** her job **up**.

short answer An answer to a *Yes/No* question that has *yes* or *no* plus the subject and an auxiliary verb.

A: Do you speak Chinese?
B: **Yes, I do. / No, I don't.**

simple past A verb form that expresses actions and situations that were completed at a definite time in the past.

Carol **ate** lunch.   She **was** hungry.

simple present A verb form that expresses general statements, especially about habitual or repeated activities and permanent situations.

Every morning I **catch** the 8:00 bus.
The earth **is** round.

social modals Modal auxiliaries that are used to express politeness, formality, and authority.

Would you please open the window?
May I help you?
Visitors **must** obey the rules.

stative verb A type of verb that is not usually used in the continuous form because it expresses a condition or state that is not changing. **Know**, **love**, **resemble**, **see**, and **smell** are some examples.

subject A noun, pronoun, or noun phrase that precedes the verb phrase in a sentence. The subject is closely related to the verb as the doer or experiencer of the action or state, or closely related to the noun that is being described in a sentence with *be*.

Erica kicked the ball.
He feels dizzy.
The park is huge.

subject relative pronoun A relative pronoun that is the subject of a relative clause. It comes before the verb in the relative clause.

the man **who** called

subordinate clause *See* **dependent clause.**

superlative A form of an adjective, adverb, or noun that is used to rank an item or situation first or last in a group of three or more.

This perfume has **the strongest** scent.
He speaks **the fastest** of all.
That machine makes **the most noise** of the three.

***that* clause** A noun clause beginning with **that.**

I think **that the bus is late.**

three-word verb A phrasal verb such as **break up with, cut down on,** and **look out for.** The meaning of a three-word verb is usually different from the individual meanings of the three words.

time clause A dependent clause that begins with a time word such as **while, when, before,** or **after.** It expresses the relationship in time between two different events in the same sentence.

Before Sandy left, she fixed the copy machine.

transitive verb A verb that is followed by an object.

I **read** the book.

two-word verb A phrasal verb such as **blow up, cross out,** and **hand in.** The meaning of a two-word verb is usually different from the individual meanings of the two words.

unreal conditional sentence A sentence that expresses an unreal situation that is not true at the present time, and its imaginary result. It has an **if** clause in the simple past and a main clause with **would** + main verb.

If I had the time, I'd walk to work.

used to A special past tense verb. It expresses habitual past situations that no longer exist.

We **used to** go skiing a lot. Now we go snowboarding.

verb A word that refers to an action or a state.

Gina **closed** the window.
Tim **loves** classical music.

verb phrase A phrase that has a main verb and any objects, adverbs, or dependent clauses that complete the meaning of the verb in the sentence.

Who **called you?**
He **walked slowly.**
I **know what his name is.**

voiced Refers to speech sounds that are made by vibrating the vocal cords. Examples of voiced sounds are /b/, /d/, and /g/.

bat **d**ot **g**et

voiceless Refers to speech sounds that are made without vibrating the vocal cords. Examples of voiceless sounds are /p/, /t/, and /f/.

u**p** i**t** i**f**

***wh-* clause** A noun clause that begins with a **wh-** word: **who, whom, what, where, when, why, how,** and **which.** Also called *indirect question* or *embedded question.*

I would like to know **where he is.**
Could you tell me **how long it takes?**

***wh-* word** Who, whom, what, where, when, why, how, and which are **wh-** words. They are used to ask questions and to connect clauses.

***wish* sentence** A sentence that has a **wish** clause in the simple present, and a simple past clause. A **wish** sentence expresses a desire to change a real situation into an unreal or impossible one.

I wish I had more time.

***Yes/No* question** A question that can be answered with the words **yes** or **no.**

Can you drive a car? Does he live here?

Index

This Index is for the full and split editions. Entries for Volume A are in bold.

object pronouns, with gerunds, 247
and reported speech, 400

Pronunciation
 of nouns ending in *-s/-es*, **A-3**
 of verbs ending in *-ed*, **A-4**
 of verbs ending in *-s/-es*, **A-3**

Proper nouns, and nonrestrictive
 relative clauses, 294

Public discourse, and passive
 sentences, 222

**Punctuation, with quoted speech,
 A-10**

Purpose infinitives, 244

Q

Questions, *see also* Indirect
 questions; **Information
 questions**; *Yes/No* questions
 with *some* and *any*, 259

Quoted speech
 punctuation with, A-10
 vs. reported speech, 394–395, 399–
 401

R

Real conditionals
 forms of, 330–334
 meaning and use of, 335–339
 and advice, warnings, and
 instructions, 336
 and certainty, 335–336
 and predictions and promises, 336
 with *unless* vs. *if*, 339

realize, **and instant events, 89**

really, **in informal speech, 22**

**Reasons, and past perfect and past
 perfect continuous, 136**

Receiver, in passive vs. active
 sentences, 198–199

recently
 **and present perfect continuous,
 109**
 and recent past time, 88, 91

Recent past time
 and adverbs, 91
 and past perfect, 130
 and present perfect, 88, 89
 **and present perfect continuous,
 109, 114**

regret, with gerunds and infinitives,
 239

Regrets
 and past modals, 181
 and wishes, 345
 past wishes, 363

**Relationships, and stative meaning,
 17**

Relative clauses, 279–324, *see also*
 Nonrestrictive relative clauses;
 Relative clauses with object
 relative pronouns; Relative clauses
 with subject relative pronouns;
 Restrictive relative clauses

Relative clauses with object relative
 pronouns, 301–324
 forms of, 304–308
 nonrestrictive relative clauses,
 305–308, 313–314
 relative clauses ending or
 beginning with prepositions,
 313–316
 restrictive relative clauses, 304,
 305–308, 313–314
 meaning and use of, 309–312,
 317–324
 nonrestrictive relative clauses,
 310, 317
 restrictive relative clauses, 309,
 317–318
 when and *where* in, 320

Relative clauses with subject relative
 pronouns, 279–300
 forms of, 282–287
 nonrestrictive relative clauses, 283
 restrictive relative clauses, 282,
 283
 meaning and use of
 nonrestrictive relative clauses,
 294–300
 restrictive relative clauses, 288–
 293

Relative pronouns, *see* Object relative
 pronouns; Subject relative
 pronouns

remember, with gerunds and
 infinitives, 239

Repeated actions, 12
 habits, 12, 13, 336
 and indefinite past time, 85
 and past perfect, 136
 and present perfect, 114
 routines, 12, 336
 schedules, 12

Reported speech, 391–409
 forms of, 394–398
 meaning and use of, 399–409
 and adverbs, 401
 and point of view, 399, 400, 401
 and pronouns and possessive
 adjectives, 400–401
 and reporting verbs, 395, 396,
 402, 404
 and tense, 399, 400

Reporting verbs, 395, 396, 402, 404,
 A-9

Requests, 58

Restrictive relative clauses
 forms of
 relative clauses with object relative
 pronouns, 304, 305, 307, 313–
 316
 relative clauses with subject
 relative pronouns, 282, 283
 meaning and use of, 288–293
 and identifying nouns, 288–289,
 305
 vs. nonrestrictive relative clauses,
 295
 reduction of, 289, 317–318

Result clauses, 335–336, 340–341,
 343, 359–360

Results, and passive sentences, 202

right now, **and present continuous, 13**

Routines
 and real conditionals, 336
 and simple present, 12

S

say
 with *regret*, 239
 as reporting verb, 396, 402

Scheduled events, 62

Schedules, and simple present, 12

**Sensations, and stative meaning, 17,
 18**

Senses, and stative meaning, 17, 18

Sentences, *see* Active sentences;
 Combining sentences; Passive
 sentences

Sequence of events, *see* Order of
 events

-s/-es (for plural)
 pronunciation of nouns with, A-3
 spelling of nouns with, A-2

Grammar Sense

ONLINE PRACTICE

How to Register for Grammar Sense Online Practice

Follow the steps to register for *Grammar Sense Online Practice*.

1. Go to www.grammarsensepractice.com and click on [**Register**]

2. Read and agree to the terms of use. [**I Agree.**]

3. Enter the Access Code that came with your Student Book. Your code is written on the inside back cover of your book.

   [ ] [ ] [ ] [ ]   [**Enter**]

4. Enter your personal information (first and last name, email address, and password).

5. Click on the Student Book that you are using for your class.

   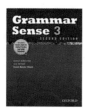

   > It is very important to select your book. You are using Grammar Sense 3. Please click the **RED** Grammar Sense 3 cover.

   If you don't know which book to select, **STOP**. Continue when you know your book.

6. Enter your class ID to join your class, and click NEXT. Your class ID is on the line below, or your teacher will give it to you on a different piece of paper.

   _____   [**Next**]

   You don't need a class ID code. If you do not have a class ID code, click Skip. To enter this code later, choose Join a Class from your Home page.

7. Once you're done, click on Enter Online Practice to begin using *Grammar Sense Online Practice.*

   [**Enter Online Practice**]

Next time you want to use *Grammar Sense Online Practice*, just go to www.grammarsensepractice.com and log in with your email address and password.